The Woman Who Walked to Russia

The Woman Who Walked to Russia

A Writer's Search for a Lost Legend

BY

CASSANDRA
PYBUS

Four Walls Eight Windows
New York/London

Published in the United States by
Four Walls Eight Windows
39 West 14th Street
New York, NY 10011
http://www.4w8w.com

First published in Canada by Thomas Allen Publishers
First U.S. printing December 2003

ISBN 1-56858-290-0 (pb)

Catalog-in-Publication Data for this book
has been filed with the Library of Congress

Printed in the United States

Interior design by Gordon Robertson
Photo of Lillian Alling courtesy of the Atlin Historical Society
Map by John Lightfoot

10 9 8 7 6 5 4 3 2 1

For Linda and Esta Spalding

"Ravens are, it seems, one of Australia's few successful animal exports, and their extraordinary world-girdling journey began on that southern continent at least 35 million years ago. It led them first to Eurasia, then via Beringia into North America and finally some two to five million years ago in South America, giving them a global distribution."

TIM FLANNERY

The Eternal Frontier: An Ecological History of North America and Its Peoples

Acknowledgements

Foremost I must thank my husband, Michael Lynch, and mother, Betty Pybus, for enduring this obsession with such good grace; also the Literature Fund of the Australia Council for their financial support.

For their unstinting help in archival matters, thanks to Suzanne den Ouden in the Yukon Archives in Whitehorse, Michael Carter in the British Columbia Archives in Victoria, and Diane Smith in the Atlin Historical Society.

For friendship and hospitality during my various trips to Canada and the United States, thanks to Alma Lee, Sara Dowse, Peter McAllister, Linda Spalding and Michael Ondaatje, Ronald Wright and Janice Boddy, and my agent, Bella Pomer. And a special thanks to the Banff Arts Centre for giving me a residency in the glorious writer's studio where this book was begun.

Finally, my heartfelt appreciation for the work of the great Haida artist Bill Reid, and all the indigenous people of the Pacific Northwest whose stories of the trickster Raven have given me much inspiration and pleasure.

PART ONE

Looking for Lillian

I

PART TWO

Raven Road

45

PART THREE

Adrift in Beringia

147

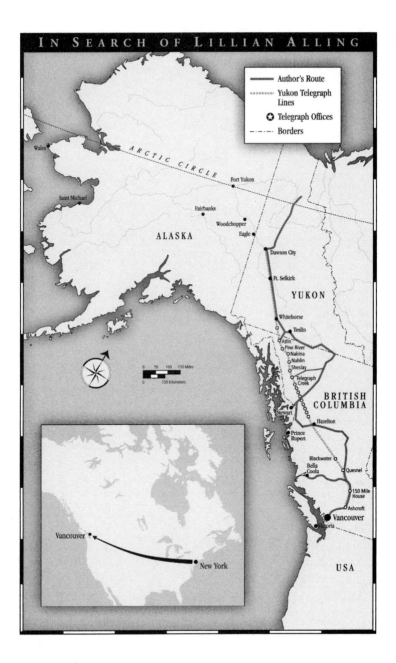

IN SEARCH OF LILLIAN ALLING

PART ONE

Looking
for Lillian

Walking to Siberia

The dog was dancing about, furiously barking in the direction of the forest south of the clearing. Bill Blackstock narrowed his eyes to make out any movement within the dark pines that would indicate a cause for alarm. If it were a wolf or a cougar, the dog would be backed against the cabin, whining, the hair bristling along her spine. Coyotes did not bother her, and it was too late in the season for bears. The weather had turned. For days the high peak of Mount Kisgegas had been shrouded in snow clouds, and beyond the forest snow had settled onto Groundhog Range. Pretty soon he could start setting his traplines.

As the telegraph operator in number two relay cabin, Blackstock was at home in the isolation of this wilderness outpost beside the churning, silt-laden Skeena River. He relished company, though, and with the small trading post of Hazelton a day's walk away, he did get visitors from time to time—hunters and fishermen mostly—though not in mid-September. And word usually preceded visitors. The operator at the first relay cabin played Blackstock at checkers over the line and always sent a message if company was on the way. There had been no wire.

Moving into the forest, he became aware of a slight figure slumped against a tree, almost obscured by the dark shadows.

An Indian child? This place had once been a Tsimshian village, and Blackstock was aware that they crept back from time to time, maybe to commune with their ancestors whose carved totems lay scattered about. He tried out a few words of Tsimshian but the figure didn't stir. Coming closer, his dog brought to heel, he realized with shock it was a white woman, her clothes disintegrating, her boots torn and gaping. Blackstock came right up to her and she didn't utter a sound when he bent down to look. She was breathing harshly and was utterly stupefied. It was impossible to tell her age. He hoisted the woman, light as feather down, under his arm. She weakly murmured protest as he carried her back to his cabin.

A foreign woman, Blackstock guessed, from the thickly accented voice. What in Lord's name was she doing in this wilderness of mountains and forest, miles from anywhere?

The woman was not injured, as Blackstock had first surmised, just bleeding from scratches where the tree stumps had torn her legs. He revived her with a shot of rum and spooned into her mouth some of the caribou stew he kept on the fuel stove. She gave him to understand that she had followed the trail cleared for the telegraph. Producing a battered, hand-drawn map, she indicated a line snaking up through the Yukon and across Alaska to the Bering Sea.

"No, ma'am," Blackstock explained, doing his best to placate his agitated guest, "the line don't go that far. Telegraph stops at Dawson City." He tapped a stubby forefinger at a point about halfway on her map.

When she made moves to gather up the ragged coat that was drying by the stove, it was apparent to Blackstock that this frail lunatic was determined to set off again to walk to Russia. Lord only knew how she'd got this far. From way back east, best as he could judge. In her weakened condition and with winter closing in, Blackstock knew she could never make it to Siberia. She wouldn't make it to the next cabin. He entreated her to rest beside the roaring stove. While she dozed in his stifling kitchen, Blackstock tapped out a telegraph message to the police in Hazelton to come and take her away.

Who was this woman who emerged out of the British Columbia wilderness in September 1927? She was said to be Lillian Alling, an immigrant in her early thirties who had arrived from Russia in New York City. Desperate with homesickness, she had haunted the New York Public Library, studying the maps and atlases to establish the most direct route home. She may not have had good English, but she did understand the hieroglyphics of cartography. In the spring of 1927, aided only by a roughly accurate, hand-drawn route map, she had set her face toward Siberia and started to walk.

It was probably in the library that she got the idea that a telegraph ran across the subarctic to the Bering Sea, unaware that the line drawn on the map represented a leap of imagination: the route of the Collins Overland Telegraph, conceived in 1865 as a visionary scheme to connect North America with Europe by way of Russian Alaska and Siberia.

The Collins Overland Telegraph was begun but never completed. Starting from Quesnel in British Columbia, axemen cut a trail as far as Teslin Lake in the Yukon, closely followed by a crew who sank the postholes and strung the wire. At the opposite end, in Eastern Siberia, a second crew of under-equipped men struggled in the face of a severe famine to sink postholes into permafrost "hard as Pharaoh's heart," while on the frozen tundra of Russian Alaska a third crew worked in cold so extreme it froze the whisky in the bottles and caused their crowbars to snap.

This monumental effort was to no avail. The project was abruptly abandoned a year later when the transatlantic cable made the concept redundant. Although the telegraph was revived at the turn of the century, in the wake of the Yukon gold rush, it was never extended beyond the subarctic township of Dawson City. Between Dawson and the Bering Sea remained an unbroached wilderness, as cruel and inhospitable as it had proved to be to the men of the Collins Overland Telegraph.

It is a mystery how Lillian managed to get all the way from New York to a point in British Columbia where she could connect with the telegraph line. Constable Wyman of the British Columbia Provincial Police had no success in establishing where the woman had come from, although he formed the opinion that she had been walking from the east. Perhaps she had followed the railway line across the states of Pennsylvania, Wisconsin, Minnesota and North Dakota, before crossing into Canada near Moose Jaw, Saskatchewan. If that were so, she must have continued along the railway northwest, climbing up into the Rockies and through Yellowhead Pass at 1,066 metres above sea level, then descended along the course of the Fraser River into British Columbia. Awesome, wild country, a challenge for the fittest and best equipped of adventurers. This woman was neither appropriately outfitted for such a rough trek nor was she robust, weighing only fifty kilograms. She may have ridden the train illegally, as so many were to do in later years when the Depression settled on America. She may even have had money for a train ticket.

Constable Wyman's concern was not how this obsessed woman had got so far; his pressing need was to dissuade her from proceeding any farther. After ascertaining her name was Lillian Alling, Wyman tried to sort out where she was heading. It took some prompting, but he finally made sense of what Lillian was trying to tell him.

"I go to Siberia," he understood her to say.

Convinced that hers was a suicidal project, Constable Wyman felt obliged to make sure that the woman stayed put. He charged her with vagrancy.

On 21 September 1927 the Hazelton police court sentenced Lillian Alling to a $25 fine or two months in prison for vagrancy and for carrying an offensive weapon, which was the way Justice of the Peace Mr. Grant chose to describe the thin iron bar she had concealed in her clothes. Of course he was doing her a favour, in his mind, stopping her walking north into the face of the subarctic winter, with its terrible blizzards and hungry wolves. She had only two $10 notes and couldn't pay the fine, so she was forced into the Oakalla prison farm outside Vancouver to sit out the winter. She would not have thanked Grant for it. The Oakalla prison farm was no rest home. She would have had to work in the prison gardens and suffer the bullying and forced intimacies of the inmates with no iron bar to fend them off.

If Grant hoped a spell in prison would dissuade the woman from her foolhardy mission, he was mistaken. As soon as summer began, she was on her way north once again, probably following the Fraser River valley, which forms a natural corridor into the Cariboo country of the interior, where the Yukon Telegraph branched west toward Hazelton.

The Yukon Telegraph had taken up where the Collins Overland Telegraph had left off when it was abandoned in

1867. The trail was still there, some thirty-five years later, for the Yukon Telegraph to follow as far as Atlin in British Columbia; from there they cut a new trail across the Yukon border to Whitehorse, where the telegraph met up with a cable being run south from the gold-rush boom town of Dawson City. This mammoth undertaking was one of the last greatest wilderness construction projects in North America.

Even with the trail cleared for the telegraph, travelling over this country would have been really tough. Sergeant Fairburn at Smithers, B.C., heard that Lillian was headed back that way at the end of June 1928, although he had not expected to see her before August. He was astonished when she turned up on 19 July. She had been walking about fifty kilometres a day, taking advantage of the long hours of daylight. Lacking an excuse to stop her, Fairburn allowed Lillian to continue northward, with instructions to report at every relay cabin along the telegraph.

For the relay men on the telegraph line, Lillian's trek must have been a marvellous diversion from the lonely humdrum of their days. Their reports on her progress make it possible to chart her trek to Atlin and then as far as Dawson City, Yukon, where the telegraph line ran out.

As did news of Lillian Alling.

The last documented sighting was in Dawson City, in May 1929, when she reportedly set out in a boat to sail the length of the treacherous Yukon River to where it empties into the Bering Sea.

I first heard about this compulsive pedestrian a few years ago when I was travelling through Northern British Columbia.

While browsing in a bookshop in Prince George, I noticed a reference to a woman who walked to Russia, just one of many remarkable tales of endurance and determination that make up the folklore of this spectacular, wild region. Masculine tales for the most part, these stories belong to the genre of heroic self-improvement: carving out new territory, striking it rich, that sort of thing. Lillian's story intrigued me in a way that the others did not, because of the intensely *domestic* impulse that fuelled her extraordinary feat. She had simply wanted to go home.

The initial information I had about her trek came from a book by Edward Hoagland, *Notes from the Century Before*, which told me that Lillian had walked the telegraph line as far as Atlin, where she spent a winter cooking for miners before heading north in the summer. According to Hoagland, she was last seen pushing off on a raft into the Bering Sea at Point Barrow, Alaska. Once I started making inquiries, I found that next to no documentation was available to corroborate this story, and I began to doubt the authenticity of Hoagland's tale.

But not before Lillian Alling had sunk her hooks into my imagination.

I couldn't stop thinking about her. Walking. All that way. In such incredible terrain and such abominable weather. All my rational responses told me she could never have done it, but I wanted so much to believe that she had.

I found a more reliable account of Lillian's trek in an article in a 1972 *True West* magazine, by veteran journalist Francis Dickie, who had pieced together bits and pieces about Lillian to create a credible narrative. Hoagland's information was wrong in almost all its particulars, I discovered. Lillian had not in fact stayed in Atlin. She had merely passed through on her way to Whitehorse. Nor was there any evidence whatsoever that she had been seen pushing off on a raft from the Alaskan coast.

Dickie was not able to say with any certainty what had happened to Lillian. The evidence he cited for her having got to Siberia was as insubstantial as a snow flurry: an Inuit hunter was said to have told some unnamed person that he saw a woman pulling a two-wheeled cart, somewhere beyond Teller, in Alaska. If such a woman had been sighted and if it were Lillian, Dickie surmised, then she was heading for the Alaskan village of Wales, opposite the Diomedes Islands, the closest point to Russia.

At the end of his article, Dickie had added a postscript that made my heart leap. He reported that after he had first written about Lillian, he had received a letter from a man named Arthur Elmore in California, who recounted the story a Russian friend had told to him in 1965. Elmore's Russian friend had spent his childhood in Siberia, and he had a vivid memory of an incident in the autumn of 1930, when he had been loitering at the Providenija waterfront and his eye was caught by a group of Diomede Inuit being interrogated by security police. Moving closer, he saw that one of the group was a Caucasian woman, dressed in Inuit furs but speaking Russian. She was trying to persuade the police that she had walked from America; that she had come home to Russia because in America she could not make friends and she had been hurt by the indifference of her new country. The journey had been long and hard, she told the police. "I did it," he clearly heard her say. The group had been taken away by the police. He never saw the woman again.

Elmore said his friend had told him this story because he had found the woman's account of herself so extraordinary that he never forgot it. Elmore himself had been haunted by his friend's tale until, seven years later, he had picked up a copy of *True West*, and all was explained.

At least, in his mind.

I wanted to believe all of this. It appealed to the storyteller in me.

My historian's inclination was to be gravely skeptical.

There was no time to pursue the case. By then I was on the last leg of my return journey to my home in southeast Tasmania, which was about as far away as was possible. Just a hop, step and a jump to the end of the world.

Once I was back in my cottage in Lower Snug, Tasmania, the story of the woman who walked to Russia continued to niggle in my mind, until I put it down on paper.

When my essay "Reaching Atlin" was published, I told myself that I had written Lillian Alling out of my system.

Beyond the Pale

Stories have a disarming way of remaking themselves.

I had woven Lillian's inconclusive tale into an essay, hoping to exorcise my obsession, but this effort only intensified the itch to know more about her. Strangers accosted me at writers' festivals or walked up to my table in restaurants, demanding to know more. I got letters asking how I could leave the story dangling in thin air. Newspaper reviewers chastised me for having whetted their appetite for Lillian's journey and then not gone the whole way.

I knew they had a point.

"Do you suppose Lillian had sex with those men on the telegraph line?" my editor asked me one day, quite out of the blue, when we were working on an unrelated project.

She too had been puzzling over how Lillian had managed to do it.

What had she eaten to stay alive? How had she avoided catastrophe?

These questions had nagged at me for some time. They still nagged at me, right down to the simple matter of her name.

Lillian Alling did not sound Russian to me. Maybe that was how Constable Wyman heard her name when she said it. Perhaps he decided that the woman was Russian because she was heading for Siberia. Could that have been her real name?

I paid a visit to the genealogical research section of my local library to search a dictionary of Russian surnames. I could find neither Alling nor Ailing. The closest name was Alenik, a variation of Olejnik, said to be a name from Belorussia (White Russia) meaning "oil presser." Variations of this name could be found clustered in a discrete geographical area between Eastern Poland, Belorussia and Lithuania: such names as Aleinikov, Alenjev, Aleinik, Olinik, Elijnikov, Olinski.

Disappointed, I made inquiries at the information desk, and the librarian in charge set me up at a computer with a stack of CD-ROMs of genealogical databases, suggesting that I start with the mother of all such databases, from the Church of the Latter-day Saints. We were both surprised when I drew a blank on Alling and Ailing; likewise, the U.S. naturalization records for New York were no help. I combed through the U.S. Social Security Death Index and the First World War military records without ever finding those surnames. The ever-helpful librarian directed me to try the

Internet and wrote down for me the Web addresses of the
big genealogical sites.

Hunched over my laptop until midnight, I found only
one family in New Jersey with the name I was searching for,
and this family had migrated from Norway in 1887. Cross-
checking with other genealogical sites, I was excited to find
that they had a daughter named Lillian, born in New Jersey
in 1896, which made her just the right age to be my elusive
quarry. Unhappily for me, this Lillian Alling had married
another Norwegian, named Alfred Jensen, in 1920 and died
in New Jersey in 1975. Pursuing my search the following
evening, I found that a related name, Ayling, was not uncom-
mon in New England, but the origin of this name was English and dated from the seventeenth century.

I also found that several of the genealogy Web sites had
a function called Soundex, which allowed me to search for
names with a similar sound. I tried this out on several databases and found Elling, Allenick, Alienikov, Alenik, Olenick,
Olenjnik, Elnik, Olejnik. Against these names were the e-mail
addresses of people with specific research interests. To each
one I sent a general inquiry, about thirty or forty messages.
Within forty-eight hours I had a multitude of responses,
from all over the United States, from Canada, from England,
from Israel and from South Africa. Despite the wide geographic spread of my contacts, their responses were almost
always the same: the ancestor they were each researching had
migrated from Russia or Poland between 1885 and 1938. With
a highlighter pen, I marked the towns from which the immigrants had come on the map of Eastern Europe. Soon I had a
dense sea of lolly pink in one particular area within a 150-
kilometre radius of the city of Minsk, in the central province
of Belarus, formerly Belorussia.

No matter what source I tapped, the answer came back the same.

My friendly librarian rang me to say that following our inconclusive search she had checked the sources of the Library of Congress, which include the records of seventy thousand people who conducted business with the Russian consulates in the United States between 1849 and 1926. By then I was quite sanguine when told that there was no record of the name I was seeking and that the nearest names were all variations on the oil presser from Belorussia: Olejnik, Olanik, Oelinik, Olinik, Olynik, Ulnik, Aleijnik and Aleynik.

What was most intriguing to me about all this information was that, in every instance, the names were those of Jewish immigrants. This was unexpected.

Back in the genealogy section of the library, I consulted all the books on Jewish names. Sure enough, all those names were sourced to the Pale of Settlement, that area between the Baltic Sea and the Black Sea where Czar Nicholas I ordered the Jews confined from in 1835. Belorussia lay at the heart of the Pale of Settlement and its Jewry made up nearly sixty per cent of the population of the principal cities of the region, giving it one of the greatest concentrations of Jews in czarist Russia. Another book that located Jewish surnames from the Russian Empire pinpointed the names to various cities in Belorussia, such as Grodno, Orsha, Vitebek, Brest, Pinsk and Minsk.

I devoured Russian history books, which told me that the further tightening of social and economic restrictions on Jews in 1881 began a massive exodus westward into Poland and the Baltic states, with the ultimate destination being the

United States of America. The flight dramatically intensified when a wave of anti-Jewish pogroms, consummated with a singular barbarity, swept across Russia between 1901 and 1917. Not all were as terrible as the 1903 pogrom in Kishinev, which left three hundred dead, many thousands wounded, and forty thousand people without property or means of work, but few towns in the Pale of Settlement escaped vengeful Russians wielding sabres. In one week during October 1905, three hundred pogroms took place in cities and towns throughout the Pale. Photographs of victims laid out in pitiful rows display hideous wounds to heads and hands inflicted by sabres and axes.

Prior to 1917, the Belorussian cities of Minsk, Gomel and Mogilev had all experienced obscene anti-Jewish outbursts, but much worse was to come with the bitter civil war that followed the Bolshevik Revolution, which saw 150,000 Jews killed. After the Treaty of Brest-Litovsk, Belorussia became a battlefield for the Red Army and the Polish and White Russian armies. Jews were killed indiscriminately, either on the charge of helping the Red forces or merely as the target of irrational resentment by both sides.

News from America boasting of boundless opportunities ricocheted around the traumatized shtetls and towns of Belorussia. Glowing stories about the successes of earlier emigrants were circulated from hand to hand, providing the basis for faith in a better life. Letters were read over and over till they were known by heart. Even children's lullabies sang the praises of America and conjured images of a land of plenty. The promise of America, combined with a gnawing fear of pogroms and the desperate need to find a way of earning a living, was sufficient inducement for Jews to risk appalling privation and danger to flee illegally across Poland to the

German ports of Hamburg and Bremen. Another route was through the Baltic states to Danzig and Riga.

Rarely was it possible for an entire family to emigrate at the same time. The father usually left first, but as time went on, it became more common to send working-age daughters. At least three-quarters of the working women in the Pale of Settlement were employed in some branch of the sewing trade. Unmarried needleworkers were readily swallowed up by the unregulated sweatshops of the garment industry in Lower Manhattan.

This, I suspect, was how Lillian came to New York City.

Rose Cohen, a young emigrant from a shtetl in Belorussia, provides a window onto this experience in her autobiography, *Out of the Shadow: A Russian Jewish Girlhood on the Lower East Side*. She was smuggled across the Polish border with her unmarried aunt, and travelled steerage from Hamburg to New York, where she worked in a small sweatshop that employed two women and six men stitching the underlining of men's coats. When Cohen arrived in New York, she spoke only Yiddish. The first English words she learned were "Keep your hands off me, please."

Since the late nineteenth century, the main gateway to the United States had been through Hamburg. Seeing the exodus of Jews as a way to fill up the steerage of their ships, agents from the Hamburg-America Line ran specifically targeted advertising campaigns in the Pale of Settlement.

Once the emigrants had made it as far as Hamburg, they needed to obtain an entry visa from a consular office and a ticket to travel steerage to the United States. Prior to departure, steerage passengers were housed and fed by a Hamburg steamship company; they were also stripped en masse and deloused and their personal clothing was disinfected.

Steerage class was in one of the three enclosed lower decks of the ship: vast sex-segregated dormitories with about two thousand metal-frame berths, extending the entire breadth of the ship, without windows and practically without ventilation or lighting, alive with lice, and rank with the smell of dirty bodies and the stench of the nearby toilets. Throughout the entire trip, the floor was slippery with vomit. Steerage was so named because it was located near the rudder, so passengers lived with the roll and thud of the waves as well as the cacophony of thousands of other miserable souls. Food consisted primarily of potatoes and salt fish collected from the ship's canteen in a bucket, although many also carried their own ethnic foodstuffs that added to the odoriferous atmosphere.

Few cared to remember that excruciating journey, which lasted about ten days. Some thought it was a purgatory that cleansed them of sin and prepared them, as if born again, to be taken into the bosom of America, embodied in the serene woman whose torchlight greeted them at the entry to New York.

> Give me your tired, your poor,
> Your huddled masses yearning to breathe free,
> The wretched refuse of your teeming shore.
> Send these, the homeless, tempest-tossed to me,
> I lift my lamp beside the golden door!
> (Emma Lazarus, "The New Colossus")

This flood of refuge seekers from Eastern Europe had a dramatic impact on the demography of the United States. In

1860 there were a hundred thousand Jews in America, and the number had more than doubled by 1880. In the next quarter of a century, almost a million more would arrive, and in a final surge between 1905 and 1927 the Jewish population rose to nearly four and a half million. Some seventy per cent of this last wave of immigrants came from Russia, the largest single group from Belorussia. By 1921 the surge was reduced to a trickle, when literacy tests and a quota system severely restricted immigration from Eastern Europe. Still, the door remained open.

I was confident that Lillian was among the few thousand Jewish immigrants still arriving in America from Belorussia in the 1920s, and that her name was probably a variation of Olejnik.

Here was every good reason for her *not* to want to return to Russia. Once Jewish emigrants made the momentous decision to leave, there was little thought of ever returning to a homeland where they were unwanted and unprotected. Compared with a return rate of around sixty per cent for Hungarian, Slovak and Italian immigrants, the estimated return rate for Eastern European Jews was a mere two per cent. It would have been next to zero in 1927–29, which was the period when Stalinist repression against the Soviet Jews was in full swing, with large-scale executions and deportations.

I found it almost impossible to believe that Lillian Alling would have wanted to go back to such a place.

Whatever could she have been up to?

The Isle of Tears

The chance to test out my speculations about Lillian came in the fall of 1997, when I was invited to a conference at the University of Massachusetts.

A short detour took me to New York City, where close friends had asked me to stay with them in the large loft they had sublet in SoHo. I caught the Peter Pan bus from Amhurst to Manhattan, driving through forests of maple that were glowing like charcoal embers in the slanting afternoon light. As we crossed the George Washington Bridge into the treeless squalor of the Bronx, the traffic began to pack down into an immobilized snarl. Around us the air was thick with smog that all but obliterated the distant Manhattan skyline.

The bus moved at a glacial pace through Washington Heights, allowing me to observe that a few oak trees had managed to survive in the cracked pavements. Unlike the trees across the Hudson, the leaves here were not turning to gold but hung from the branches, shrivelled and brown, like a dismal colony of bats.

On the streets of Harlem I watched men push grocery carts containing their belongings down Malcolm X Boulevard and counted two Baptist churches in each block. Among this sea of black faces, a young white woman in a denim cap and jacket stood on the curb speaking urgently into a cellphone. Hers was the only white face I saw in more than a dozen blocks, except for blond babes languishing on billboards high above the pavement.

Once we were below 90th Street, the few black faces belonged to young women wheeling white toddlers in strollers.

For the most part, the pedestrians were pared-down women, almost wafer-thin, wearing subdued colours of black and beige; a few elongated men were speaking into cellphones. Here the dingy pavement was transformed by piles of bulbous orange pumpkins spilling out from under smart green awnings, along with massed bunches of scarlet and yellow dahlias, delicate pink lilies and bright blue hydrangeas. Here, too, the tension of the city had accelerated. On a lamppost the authorities had issued the warning DON'T HONK, threatening a $350 fine, yet all round me exasperated drivers leaned on their horns in an ear-splitting cacophony of impotent rage.

When the bus finally pulled into the Port Authority Terminal, it was more than two hours behind schedule.

In my reckless youth I had lived in this city for a time, but I had not been back for more than twenty years. As I pushed my way onto Eighth Avenue, it was instantly familiar to me: the indifferent crush of people, the fetid air and the ambient noise level, well above safe decibels.

Hideous and exhilarating.

It was probably no less so in the 1920s when Lillian arrived through the stern portals of Ellis Island.

Next morning I took a ferry from Battery Park out to a narrow sandbar at the mouth of the Hudson River, where an abandoned building in the style of the French Renaissance was all that remained of the reception centre that had once processed sixteen million immigrants. In his essay on Ellis Island, the French writer Georges Perec describes this building as "a sort of factory for manufacturing Americans, a factory for transforming emigrants into immigrants; an American-style factory, as quick and efficient as a sausage factory in Chicago. You pour an Irishman, a Ukrainian Jew, or an Italian from Apulia, in one end of the production line and at the other end—after vaccination, disinfection, an examination of his eyes and pockets—an American emerged." Even though it was a massive dumping ground where harassed clerks daily baptized Americans by the tens of thousands, for those whose new lives hung in the balance—for a few hours or sometimes for days—Ellis Island was the ultimate site of exile, where place was absent: the non-place, the nowhere. The alienation was especially profound for the children. "By the time we came to New York City," a Ukrainian youth remembered in 1921, "the experience of Ellis Island had aged us. We didn't want to sing anymore. We were all grown up."

In every European tongue, this place was named the Isle of Tears.

The immigrants arrived by ferry, carrying their bundles on their backs or their heads, with their number from the ship's manifest pinned to their coats. On the ferry, jammed so tightly they could barely manage to turn around, they waited for many hours in the heat or the cold, without food and water, before disembarking at Ellis Island, where bewildered men and women were harried into separate lines for entry procedures.

First, they had to endure rudimentary medical examinations, undertaken as the lines wound past a series of doctors probing eyes and mouths for symptoms of contagious diseases such as trachoma, typhus and tuberculosis. Any sign of these conditions meant automatic expulsion. Avrom Reisen captured this moment in his poem "The First Immigrants":

A stranger receives us
Harshly and asks: "And your health?"
He examines us. His look
Assesses us like dogs.

He studies in depth
Eyes and mouth. No doubt
That if he'd probed our hearts
He would have seen the wound.

Typically an examination might take fifteen seconds, after which the doctors chalked their diagnosis on the shoulder of any dubious case: *L* for lameness, *C* for chest complaint, *H* for heart trouble and *X* for feeble-mindedness. Individuals thus marked were detained on the island for additional hours or days or weeks while they were subjected to a more thorough examination. It was a harrowing experience, although only two per cent were ever shipped back to the countries they had fled.

Those who emerged from this examination unscathed were required to appear at one of a long row of legal desks, behind each of which sat an inspector with an interpreter. The inspectors had about two minutes in which to decide whether the immigrant had the right to enter the United States, based on a series of questions:

"What is your name?"

"Where are you from?"

"Why have you come to the United States?"

"How old are you?"

"How much money do you have?"

"Can you show it to me?"

"Who paid for your crossing?"

"Do you have any friends or family here?"

"Is there anyone who can vouch for you?"

"What kind of work do you do?"

"Are you an anarchist?"

"A polygamist?"

If any kind of problem was detected, the inspector would note "SI" on the immigrant's record, which meant that person had to undergo a far more detailed interrogation before a committee made up of three inspectors. After 1917 a literacy test was also applied. Passages from the Bible, rendered in the language of the immigrant—Hebrew, Yiddish, Persian, Russian or even Hindustani—had to be read and repeated before entry was permitted.

Few immigrants spent more than four hours on the island, but that brief time must have felt like a life sentence. At stake was a new life in America for people who had given up their past and their history, risked their lives and abandoned their kin. To be turned away after so much sacrifice was insupportable.

Three thousand immigrants took their own lives on Ellis Island.

As I wandered around Ellis Island, I imagined what it would have been like for Lillian, trudging off the crowded ferry with bundles in each hand, the manifest number pinned to her jacket and her registration card held between her teeth. Like most of the women around her, she would have been wearing the traditional headscarf and layers of extra clothing. In the wide entry hall, she would have waited to have her baggage inspected before she filed past medical inspectors

who would have peered under her eyelids for signs of trachoma, using the same buttonhook they had used for everyone else, infected or otherwise.

Presumably Lillian passed the inspection and continued
up the broad staircase, steadying herself on rails polished to
a high sheen by sixteen million anxious hands. In the bright
registration hall, light streamed through the leaded squares
of high, wide windows and was refracted by the white zigzag
tiles of the vaulted ceiling. Observed by sharp-eyed inspectors on the second-level balcony, she would have waited with
thousands of others on long, low benches, in a sweat of nervous fear, until it was her turn to be interrogated. Lillian
must have been literate in her native Yiddish to gain entry.
Almost certainly she would also have been able to read and
write in Hebrew, since a network of Hebrew schools was
long established in Belorussia. She may even have had some
English literacy, as many prospective immigrants took pains
to learn the language, to ensure they would not be turned
away as the immigration restrictions tightened.

Was this the time when Lillian anglicized her name?

The folklore of Ellis Island is replete with stories about
name changes: the man from Berlin who was dubbed Berliner;
Vladimir who was given Walter as his first name; Smilikov
who became Smiley. Prospective immigrants were often
advised to pick a truly American name that would cause no
difficulty in their new environment. Georges Perec tells the
story of an elderly Russian Jew who chose the name Rocke-
feller on the advice of a Yiddish-speaking employee in the baggage room. The old man kept repeating the name to be sure
he would get it right, but several hours later when the immigration officer asked him for his name, the stress of waiting
had driven it from his mind. He answered in Yiddish, "*Schon*

vergessen"—meaning "I've already forgotten"—and was registered with the truly American name of John Ferguson.

The story was undoubtedly apocryphal. Ellis Island authorities did not create names; they had in front of them the names on the manifest of the steamship company, listed abroad and closer to the immigrant's home. This man's name was most likely recorded with a high degree of accuracy at his European port of departure. Ellis Island officials operated under regulations that forbade them to change identifying information on the manifest, unless requested by the immigrant or unless closer inspection demonstrated that the original information was in error. Moreover, a third of all immigration inspectors were themselves foreign-born, and all of them spoke three languages. They were assigned to inspect immigrant groups based on the languages they spoke, as well as having access to an army of interpreters.

So, if it happened that Lillian's name was changed during immigration procedure, it would have been at her own behest.

Her anxious wait at Ellis Island would not necessarily have been at an end when the immigration official stamped her entry papers and welcomed her to America. The land of a thousand dreams was in sight, but if she were travelling alone she would not have been permitted to join the long queue for the ferry to Battery Park. Young women travelling alone were subject to a special kind of scrutiny, and for good reason. Bewildered, unaccompanied females were easy prey for the Jewish underworld, which made a steady profit by supplying the brothels of Latin America and Asia. In *Daughters of the Shtetl* by Susan A. Glenn, I read that half the prostitutes in Buenos Aires in 1909 were Jewish women who had come originally from the Pale of Settlement. This is why immigration officials refused to release unaccompanied women into the custody of any person who was not a relative or could not prove they were suitable guardians. Without the intervention of the Council of Jewish Women, who undertook temporary guardianship and found suitable accommodation in places like the Jewish Home for Girls on Delancey Street, women could have been stranded on Ellis Island indefinitely.

Whether or not Lillian found her first home on Delancey Street in Manhattan, she would most likely have gone to live in that vicinity. The Lower East Side was home to half a million of her countrymen and women who were employed in workshops, making clothes or cigars or reclaiming remnants from fur and leather.

There was a suggestion that Lillian had worked as a maid in New York, but this would be most unlikely. The needle trade was a respectable occupation for a Jewish woman from Belorussia, but being a maid was not. Domestic service was seen to be demeaning, and it was generally considered a tragedy if a Jewish girl became a maid. Almost certainly, Lillian would have found employment in one of the myriad of garment workshops in and around Orchard Street.

When I lived in Manhattan, I always went to Orchard Street to buy clothes from impossibly crowded little stores containing a crush of designer seconds with the labels cut off. Fabulous bargains. I still wear one of the jackets I bought in Orchard Street in 1975.

From the loft in SoHo, it was only a stroll along Broome to Delancey and then down Orchard to the old garment district. At 97 Orchard Street the National Trust for Historic Preservation was reconstituting a tenement in which generations of immigrants had lived, cheek by jowl, before it was boarded up in 1938 when the landlord decided it was not worth his while to make the improvements demanded by the city authorities. Using the material evidence of the building as well as the memories of those who had once lived there, a team of historians and archaeologists was painstakingly recreating in the Lower East Side Tenement Museum the domestic world of three different families in the three different periods between 1874 and 1938.

Each of the twenty apartments had been modified from the original design by the addition of an air shaft, a sink with cold running water and a toilet on the landing, but each remained basically the same three small rooms. While I was being shown one apartment on the first floor, I noticed on the doorway and all over the walls a cramped pencil squiggle that, on closer inspection, turned out to be orders for jackets, overcoats, dresses and shirts. In the tiny second bedroom, with a window that opened onto the grubby air shaft, was a discarded sign: PANTS MADE TO ORDER $1.50. It was my bet that in just such an apartment as this, Lillian would have worked with maybe seven or eight others, in the dim light, stitching until her arms ached, or running cloth through the Singer sewing machine.

Until she had had enough.

Until she turned her face toward the north and began to walk.

Looking for Lillian

So confident was my reconstruction of Lillian's migration experience that I had begun to form pictures of her, demure in a headscarf, bending over a pair of men's trousers in the dingy, fetid room next to the air shaft of number 97 Orchard Street.

All that remained was for me to locate the documentation. It was at this step that my reconstruction began to unravel.

The National Archives in Washington, D.C., had microfilm of the passenger manifests of every ship that came to major ports of entry in the United States, including New York, between 1820 and 1957. Using the Soundex function, I was able to check at the same time all the names with a similar sound. Casting my net as wide as possible, I searched for every Lillian I could find with a surname that sounded anything like Alling, or any of the variations I had already encountered. Scouring many, many microfilm reels containing tens of thousands of landing cards, I was able to locate fewer than a handful of possibilities. Lillian Almond was only a vague possibility, since her age on arrival was given as thirty-one. Equally, Lillian Alicant was a long shot at eight and a half, although I was taken with the possibilities of Lillian Olenick, aged seven. Toward the end of my search, I was convinced I had finally found her in Lillian Ayling, aged twenty-six. The name was correct and she was just the right age. As soon as I located this name on the faint microfilm, which was by now swimming in front of my strained eyes, I felt my heartbeat quicken.

Armed with the corresponding reel number for the manifest list, I hurried to the microfilm drawers, fumbling in my excitement. As I snatched up the appropriate reel, I was overcome with disappointment. The manifest on that reel began in October 1929, more than three years after my Lillian was arrested in British Columbia.

Refusing to be daunted, I switched my attention to Lillian Olenick, reasoning that she could have come to New

York as a child of a Yiddish-speaking family and lived in the largely Jewish ghetto of the Lower East Side, where she would not have learned to speak good English. It took me several attempts to locate the exact manifest listing for the Olenick family of five. I was confused at first by the fact that their ship came from Buenos Aires, rather than Hamburg or any other European port. I was further confused by the fact that John Olenick and his wife were described as English. Closer examination revealed that twenty years earlier, John Olenick had migrated from Europe to Canada, where all the children were born, and thence to Buenos Aires. There was no way his youngest daughter, Lillian, was my subject.

After eight hours of searching, I had nothing: Lillian Almond, who arrived in 1912, was conclusively eliminated, as was Lillian Alicant.

A further option was to search every possible surname without referring to the given name. An impossible task. I would have gone blind in the process.

The 1920 census for New York was no great help to me— even though it, too, employed Soundex—because it was too early for the period of my research. Information from the next census was not yet publicly available.

I consulted one of the young men at the reference desk, explaining that I had not been able to find my subject in the New York passenger lists, after an exhaustive search.

"What makes you sure her port of entry was New York?" he asked.

This was a very good question.

I began to realize that the story that Lillian had come from New York was probably guesswork, based on an assumption that most immigrant Russians had entered America through that gateway. Loath though I was to let go of the picture I had

constructed of her experience, I had to confess that I did not
know for sure that Lillian had arrived in America through
Ellis Island.

"Try the arrivals for Boston, Philadelphia or Baltimore. She
could very easily have come through those ports, you know."

Thankfully, Baltimore was eliminated because the national
archives did not have records for the period 1910–1954.
Boston's index yielded no one who seemed to correspond to
my elusive quarry. Philadelphia was the same.

"Of course she may have come in through Canada, a very
common route," I was told, when in despair I retreated back
to the reference desk. I was directed to more microfilm reels
that listed the details of people who had emigrated across
Canadian border points.

"Hold up," I said, rubbing my eyes in exhaustion. "Since
I know of this woman only because of information about her
in Canada, it would be downright foolishness to presume
that she had migrated from Canada into the United States
and back again."

"Then you need the Canadian immigration records."

"And where do I find them?" I asked, looking around the
marble expanse of the reading room.

"In the National Archives in Ottawa."

"Good God, I am not going up there."

"Can't say I blame you, ma'am."

Having drawn a blank on immigration records, I recalled
that one family who had lived in the tenement at 97 Orchard
Street in the 1930s had been illegal immigrants. After 1924,
immigration from Eastern Europe had virtually shut down,

and illegal entry, such as passage on a small ship that would put into an unofficial port on the eastern seaboard, was just about the only way to get a start in the land of dreams.

Perhaps I was wasting my time with official landing cards.

I determined that the most sensible strategy was to follow up the tangible elements of Lillian's story, which were her encounters with the provincial police in British Columbia and with the men who worked on the Yukon Telegraph. An Internet search revealed that this documentation could be found in the British Columbia Archives in the provincial capital of Victoria, on Vancouver Island.

I changed my return flight to travel via Vancouver rather than Los Angeles and allowed for a thirty-hour stopover.

Depositing my bags in the left luggage at Vancouver International Airport, I took a short flight to Victoria and signed on at the archives.

The records of the provincial police seemed the obvious place to start. On inquiry, I was told that the archives held only a very small portion of the provincial police records.

"How so?" I snapped, considerably miffed. "Where else would they be?"

With stoic Canadian good grace, the archivist patiently explained that when the provincial police was disestablished in the late 1940s, many of the records ended up with the successor agency, the Royal Canadian Mounted Police, or in a community museum, or, the most likely scenario, in the garbage. Together, we scanned the listing using the keyword search "provincial police." Nothing for Hazelton, where Lillian was sentenced by the Justice of the Peace. For Smithers, where Sergeant Fairburn was stationed in 1928, we found only the offence book and the provincial police court records book, 1926–54.

I was dubious about their worth but consulted them anyway.

Again, nothing.

I was then directed to look at the annual reports of the provincial police, which involved searching through microfilm of the British Columbia Sessional Papers for 1926–27. In addition to a general description of the police force, I found the annual crime statistics. They were an aggregate total for the entire province. No individual detachment provided any specific details.

In the published material held by the archives, I found a book of British Columbia Provincial Police stories but, predictably, it dealt with murders and bank robberies—nothing so small, however curious, as a woman trying to walk to Siberia. I could not even find the name of Constable Wyman.

An entirely wasted day.

Next morning I was determined to tackle the Oakalla Prison records, but I failed to find any reference to them on the computer catalogue.

I approached the desk, looking disgruntled.

The mild-mannered archivist braced himself.

"Due to the personal nature of many of these records," he told me, "most Oakalla records are restricted. Is there a particular type that you are searching for?"

"I want to see a file, or other documentation, relating to a woman sentenced for vagrancy in 1927," I told him.

The bad news was that the British Columbia government microfilmed the Oakalla records many years ago and then destroyed the originals. Unfortunately, this microfilming work was not created in accordance with modern microfilming standards, and records were so poorly ordered that it could take a considerable time to find any records, if indeed they were even filmed.

I was prepared to give it try.

The archivist grimaced when he gave me the even worse news.

"Since these records contain a great deal of personal information about named individuals, you will have to apply through the B.C. Archives' Information and Privacy Office."

He pushed a ten-page document toward me. Seven of these ten pages consisted of an application form that required me to detail—preferably type—the records requested, my research proposal, three references and a comprehensive curriculum vitae. As it happened, I could manage to complete this form because I was carrying a copy of my cv and was able to give the names and phone numbers of three academics I knew at the University of British Columbia.

Sighing deeply, I handed the form back and waited as he read it through and put it into a wire tray.

"So, can I see the records?"

"Oh dear, no." He was flustered with embarrassment. "I am sorry to have misled you. It will take thirty days for this to be approved."

I did my best to look understanding.

My flight left at nine that evening and I had the whole day in front of me. I stood at the desk entirely stumped about what to do.

"How do you know about this woman?" the archivist gently inquired.

"I have read an article about her written by a man named Francis Dickie, but I am beginning to think she was no more than a chimera."

His face broke into a broad smile, happy to be of service at last.

"Francis Dickie! He was a local journalist. Dead now. We have his papers. Metres of them."

It was true. The Archives of British Columbia did have a huge cache of letters and other material from Francis Dickie. It did not include any letters or record of interview with members of the provincial police or linesmen from the Yukon Telegraph. It did not include any reference to a woman walking to Russia. It did not include any letter from an Arthur Elmore about a story told to him by a Russian friend about a woman seen on the Providenija waterfront in 1930.

I gave up and wandered outside into the fresh air. It was not yet noon.

Victoria, with its phony English prissiness, was not a favourite place of mine, so I rang my dear friend Alma in Vancouver. We arranged to meet for an early supper near where she worked on Granville Island before I caught my plane home.

The Harbour Air seaplane from Victoria to Vancouver flew low over the Saanich Peninsula, providing a bird's-eye view of a manicured shore lined with condominiums, large gabled houses and crowded marinas. On the smaller Gulf Islands, the indented coast was pockmarked with timber-and-glass constructions perched above the log-strewn shore like monstrously deformed seabirds. A rain shower was just clearing as we approached Vancouver, leaving thin wisps of cloud caught in the top of the massive Douglas fir trees of Stanley Park. This wedge of near wilderness, which separates Burrard Inlet from English Bay, would have to be Vancouver's greatest asset. One can spend hours meandering along its soft, dank trails, through forest hundreds of years old, with no notion that it is right on the edge of a big, modern city.

Leaving the seaplane terminal on the Vancouver waterfront, I decided to skirt Stanley Park around the seawall to English Bay, which took about three hours. Bicyclists and in-line skaters whizzed past me as I walked at a steady pace, keeping hard against the seeping, fern-encrusted cliff, while out to sea a line of empty container ships, riding high in the water, swung leisurely on their anchors as if carefully choreographed. When I reached the end of the seawall, the sound of Fred Astaire started up from a loudspeaker somewhere in the park.

When they begin the beguine . . .

Irresistibly drawn toward the music, I came upon a handful of elderly couples at the edge of the park, dancing to a sound system mounted on a podium. The women were lovely in taffeta and sequins, while the men wore sombre suits. As they twirled and glided, their sole audience was a bemused raccoon who regarded them through his rakish black eye-band from under a nearby cluster of hydrangea bushes.

This delightful folly reinforced my long-standing opinion that Vancouver is one of the nicest places on earth—even though it does rain there much of the time. The city has been a magnet for people from all over the globe for a century or more, and it is one of the most polyglot places on earth. Strangely, Lillian seems to have been impervious to its manifest charms.

According to Francis Dickie's account, Lillian left the Oakalla Prison at the beginning of November 1927 and stayed in Vancouver for another eight months working in the kitchen of a restaurant, before heading north once more. Dickie does not say how he knew this, but it seems that nothing Lillian experienced in this benign, easygoing city caused her to waver in her desire to quit North America. Perhaps she felt anger toward the provincial police for having forcibly removed her to Vancouver and locked her up in a prison. Maybe this had become part of her catalogue of disillusion with the new world she had come to.

Mind you, everything about Lillian suggested to me that she was not entirely of sound mind. Had she become unhinged by loneliness and alienation?

To get across to Granville Island, I had to walk the length of English Bay to a wharf under the bridge at False Creek, where a tiny ferry bobbed over the choppy water like a child's toy. Five other tourists were waiting, happily conversing in Italian. There was just enough room inside the rotund little craft for the six of us.

Disembarked at the island, I bounded up the steps two at a time, eager for the sights and smells of the food market. A flower stall with buckets of heady, scented lilies framed the market entrance, while inside, fruit and vegetable stalls competed for display: pyramids of glossy red tomatoes and unruly heaps of shiny green peppers; bunches of sugar bananas like fists of stubby fingers; baskets stacked high with fat strawberries, and Golden Delicious apples the size of baseballs, each cradled in a nest of pastel tissue paper. In the fish section, glistening, iridescent salmon were laid out on mountains of crushed ice. After wandering up and down the aisles, intoxicated by the cornucopia, I located Alma listening to buskers in the market square.

Ignoring my insistence that I buy her almost everything on display in the market, she expertly steered me into a bar and restaurant above the congested marina and ordered two martinis: gin, not vodka, with a dash of vermouth, no ice and an olive, not a twist. I was surprised that she should have to issue precise instructions for the making of a martini. In Vancouver, I was assured, martinis came in a whole range of spirits and flavours. I had tried several exotic combinations before she bundled me into a taxi for the airport.

As well as being a literary impresario, Alma had very good connections in the burgeoning Vancouver film world. She was able to tell me that I was not the only person with an interest in Lillian Alling. At least one film script—a fictionalized account of Lillian's trek—was doing the rounds, but one producer had concluded that the story lacked dramatic tension. No love interest.

I mulled over this assessment during the tediously long trip home to Tasmania, running the basic scenario through my mind: a lone woman treks through barely penetrable wilderness and across the subarctic tundra, apparently intending to cross over the frozen sea to Soviet Russia where her own people are being slaughtered and deported, as they have been for centuries. There must have been some pretty dramatic tension to impel her to undertake such a project.

Could it have been love?

What other impulse was potent enough?

Such a Good Idea

I did my best to forget about Lillian. Other projects presented themselves, and soon she became little more than an
occasional idle thought.

Then one dazzling day in late April I took a kayak for a
paddle around my bay at Lower Snug. The water glistened
as if it had been dusted with glitter and was so perfectly
translucent that patterns of sunlight danced on the sandy
bottom. No currents stirred the two sleek yachts anchored
to moorings in the lee of the bay, nor was there a breath of
wind, yet far out I could see a dark patch seething in the
otherwise placid water. Manoeuvring the kayak toward it, I
found hundreds, if not thousands, of sooty birds, splashing
and thrashing as they feasted on a school of small fish.

This was part of the annual migration of the short-tailed
shearwater, commonly known as muttonbirds, which nest all
along the coast of eastern Tasmania. Their frenzied feeding
fattened them up for an astounding, unbroken flight all the
way to the Bering Strait to spend the winter. In the following
spring, each pair would make the epic return trip to raise one
chick in the exact same burrow they had left. A century ago, a
traveller in these parts wrote of seeing a continuous stream of
shearwaters pass across the sun, darkening the sea for a full
hour and a half as they returned unerringly to their burrows.

Something about these plucky birds, instinctively wing-
ing it all that way to Siberia, encouraged me to think that I
might make the same journey.

Resting on my paddle, I conceived the bold idea of following the trail of the enigmatic Lillian to her destination.

I had a few clues as to how this might be done.

During my previous trip to Washington, I had been introduced to a Russian academic who thought he could help me track down evidence that Lillian had arrived in Providenija. I had been greatly excited by this prospect, but after months of silence I realized that this line of inquiry was unlikely to yield me anything. Other writers who had been to Russia told me that finding information in the chaos that is the old Soviet Union could be managed only after the right people—a ubiquitous class of gangsters—had been paid off. By now my historian's appetite had been thoroughly whetted by the idea of the Soviet archives.

One thing about a police state: they keep wonderfully good records, even in a remote outpost like Providenija. What was needed was somehow to get access to the old Soviet archives.

Thinking about official Soviet records triggered some grim speculation. In 1930 Stalin's Russia was at the height of paranoia. What would have been the fate of a woman—or anyone—trying to enter from America? Surely they would have been taken for a spy. "Interrogated" was the word used by the man who claimed to have seen the woman on the waterfront of his childhood. If Lillian actually had got to Siberia, she would almost certainly have suffered some atrocious fate at the hands of Stalin's brutal security watchdogs. They would never have believed the story that she had turned her back on America and walked home.

I discussed the matter with a journalist friend who specialized in Russian affairs. He insisted that the only thing to do was to go to Siberia and get the information for myself.

I was aghast at the idea.

"You can't seriously suggest that I should go to Providenija, of all the godforsaken places."

My friend shrugged off my alarm. He had recently made a tortuous trip to the Russian Far East.

"You have to go to Providenija, Cassandra. You won't have a story otherwise." He waved his finger to silence any further protest. "I know it can be done. You fly there from Alaska."

That was all very well for him. He was a young and intrepid foreign correspondent who was employed by an international media corporation with the right connections. The word "intrepid" did not apply so readily to me: a middle-aged woman without institutional support, who didn't know quite what she was looking for.

Undaunted by my negative response, my friend supplied me with information about Providenija, which was now part of the Chukotka Autonomous Region of the Russian Far East, and he sent me the e-mail address of a small tour company in Anchorage, Alaska, which took people there.

Godforsaken, indeed.

Providenija sounded like an awful place, cut off from the rest of Siberia by the forbidding Chukotka mountain range; there were no roads from Providenija into the interior. Its sole reason for existence was as an important border post for guarding the Soviet empire against the enemy across that narrow stretch of water in America. Until 1956, Providenija was under the complete control of the notorious Gulag authorities. Nowadays it is littered with rusting tanks and discarded rolls of barbed wire, no more than a shabby echo of its Cold War importance.

A visit would not be a traveller's delight, that much was clear.

Re-energized by the example of the muttonbirds, I wrote away to the Russian Intourist organization and sent e-mails to experts on the Russian Far East. From Canada, I got survey maps that had clearly delineated the Yukon Telegraph Trail as far as Whitehorse. On these maps I could see that there were dirt roads connecting the original stations of the telegraph, the broken lines on the map suggesting that these roads were very rough and suitable only for four-wheel drive. From Whitehorse, the Klondike Highway followed the route of the telegraph all the way up to Dawson City, where another dirt road, open only in summer, grandly named the Top of the World Highway, crossed over into Alaska and ran down to Anchorage. From Anchorage, I could fly to Providenija.

To follow Lillian's trek from Vancouver would involve a return trip of ten thousand kilometres, allowing for a side trip to Providenija, and to do the trip I would need to hire a four-wheel-drive vehicle for five to six weeks.

Out of the question, really.

I rehearsed the possibilities of such a trip with my editor. She was hugely enthusiastic about the idea of following Lillian's trail and was in no mood to listen to any excuses I tried to manufacture.

"Such a long way. How could I possibly pay for it?" I moaned.

"Such a good idea," she countered. "Apply for a research grant."

My husband, Michael, took a very different tack. A trip of that nature was quite beyond a woman over fifty travelling alone, he insisted. In his opinion, driving on the wrong side of the road was hazardous enough.

"You could come with me," I said.

Michael gave me an affectionate hug. "What would I want to do that for?"

I have long since learned to interpret this phrase as a negative response, yet I persisted.

"We could have such a great time," I murmured into his shirt buttons.

"I refuse to drive on the wrong side of the road," he said, releasing me.

"And I refuse to take no for an answer."

Stubbornly I went ahead and applied for a travel grant that Michael proofread as a precaution against my dyslexic spelling. Being a pen-and-paper man, he does not trust the spell-check on my computer. In the process he discovered that my arithmetic was so incompetent that he was forced to completely recast the budget.

"Now you have a commitment to it," I chirped over his shoulder as I watched his meticulous calculations. "You'll have to come along with me."

My calculations were wrong there as well. No amount of guile will persuade Michael to do something he doesn't choose to do.

I love him for it, but there are times I would welcome a bit more plasticity, as on this occasion when I was trying to translate my research grant into a project.

The only opportunity I had to make the trip was in August and September, just before the big freeze set in. An international conference on climate change fell right in the middle of that time, and Michael had been appointed to the organizing committee.

"This is about saving the planet," he offered by way of softening his refusal to accompany me. "We'll just have to go careering across Alaska to Siberia some other time."

I had spent days and nights poring over maps and organizing the tortuous logistics for this trip. I could not imagine another time.

Planning was well advanced. I had negotiated a good deal for a rental vehicle from August to September—apart from the outrageous insurance premium—and had booked a trip to Providenija through a company in Anchorage. My friend Alma, in Vancouver, had been deputized to purchase an icebox and a Tranjia stove from a camping supply shop. In a notebook, I had written down all the foodstuffs I would need to buy from the wonderful Granville Island Market, right down to the ingredients for harissa sauce. On the right-hand pages of the notebook, I had listed the desired destination for each day, the possible accommodation, gas stations and emergency phone numbers. From the Internet I had downloaded descriptions of the dirt roads I was to travel, and had scanned fishing and hunting Web sites to locate every cabin with kitchen facilities in the vicinity of the route. The left-hand page was blank, to write the daily menus.

I was ravenous for the experience. I wanted to go then, not sometime in the future.

Just as I was thrashing around, refusing to totally abandon the idea, I received an unexpected e-mail from an old friend who had found my home page while surfing the Internet in Galveston, Texas.

It was like an answered prayer.

PART TWO

Raven
Road

Pine Resort

"Come for the murder, have you?" A woman of indeterminate age peers at me through the insect screen of the plywood office beneath brooding pines.

I knew something like this would happen once I realized that this place was nowhere to be found on my map of British Columbia. The narrow dirt road had become increasingly rutted, and there was something uncanny about the way the dark trees had closed in on both sides. Weird signs with coded messages were nailed to their trunks.

"Well, have you?" The woman behind the screen is still waiting.

Seeking reassurance, I shoot a nervous look toward Gerry, my long-lost friend from Galveston, but she is slumped exhausted over the wheel of our Nissan Pathfinder. "We, um, we were looking for a cabin for the night. Two people."

"Oh, sure," she breaks into a big-hearted grin. Out of the door now, she leads me down to a collection of tatty cabins overlooking a limpid, tea-coloured lake. "Thought you were one of the murder mystery party from Pemberton. They camp here every year."

"Murder mystery?"

"My word. It's a big deal round these parts. Didn't you see their clues on the trees along the road? People make a weekend of it." We stop outside a cabin near the lake while she fumbles with some keys. "Where you folks from?"

"Australia. Well, I'm from Tasmania, actually."

"How about that? I wish I could go to Tasmania."

"Me too," I say wearily.

The airy cabin is set up for fishermen, with a communal bathhouse and toilet off somewhere in the trees. I take it without a second glance. The sleeping arrangements are rudimentary—mattress, pillow and blanket—but it beats sleeping out among the unsettling pines, which is what Gerry had suggested. We've got sleeping bags, all right, but I swore off sleeping on the ground when I turned forty.

I go back to the car and tell Gerry to bring in the sleeping bags while I carry in the big box of food bought at the Granville Island Market. I spent the best part of yesterday purchasing wonderful delicacies to tide us over the culinary disaster zone we were about to enter. From Australia I have carried my favourite small kitchen knife, a lemon squeezer and a pepper grinder. I am determined to eat well on this trip, rather than resort to the horrible fast food of roadside diners.

Now I am ravenous, practically salivating with hunger.

"For dinner we'll have risotto. With pesto and shaved Parmesan," I call out, unpacking fresh mushrooms, arborio rice, a tub of homemade chicken stock and a pot of hydroponic basil.

"Not for me," Gerry replies from the porch. "I'm not hungry." She strikes a light to her cigarette. "You eat it, Cassandra. I can see you really like your food."

After a few deep draws, she stubs out the cigarette, jerks off her T-shirt and sprints to the dock on the lake, from which she swims to a waterslide moored in the middle of the lake. Her style is clumsy. Growing up in arid Australia, away from the coast, she had only dams and waterholes to swim in, so she never really got the hang of the Aussie crawl. Sleek as an otter, she scrambles up the slide and shoots into the water, arms akimbo, landing with a massive splash. Her delighted whoop rings out across the still water. Time and time again, she repeats the action with all the abandon of a child.

It has been such a long while since I last saw Gerry.

She and I met up two days ago in Vancouver, after we had agreed over e-mail that she would be my driver up to Alaska. She had just finished a stint on the oil rigs in the Gulf of Mexico and was looking for adventure. Working on oil rigs was just one of a number of strange jobs she has had, here, there and everywhere: coal mining, constructing walking trails, trapping feral cats. Really tough work. Gerry was an amazing young woman, strong and fearless.

Maybe not so young. Ten years younger than I am made her over forty now.

We had been close friends more than twenty years ago, when I was at a loose end in my life, dawdling through my Ph.D., doing just about anything rather than put pen to paper and working part-time in the kitchen of an inner Sydney wine bar. It was the one time in my adult life when I was completely on my own, having just walked out on my lover of eight years. Gerry was working at the bar. I found her earthy irreverence and exuberance to be a breath of fresh air after the high-octane intellectualism of the life I had abandoned.

Tall, fair and big-boned, she was a bit of a Valkyrie, according to the awe-struck manager of the wine bar, whom she dismissed as a simpering fart. Travelling through India, Gerry had developed a flair for spices, so I arranged for her to help me in the kitchen. The menus got hotter and more aromatic. We had a great time together: chopping and chattering and swigging wine. By the time the lunch orders had finished, we were very nearly pie-eyed.

In those days she rode a big, black Honda motorbike. Although she was only nineteen, she was completely in command of that monster.

One glorious spring day when work had finished for the week, we shovelled the leftovers of the jambalaya into a container, which we stowed with a wine cask and our sleeping bags in the panniers of the bike, and took off south to the national park. As the wind whipped my face with the pungent aroma of new eucalyptus, I leaned into her strong back and clung on for dear life.

We made camp under an unbroken sky ablaze with stars, smoked a few joints and polished off the wine while we tried to identify various constellations in the dazzling heavens above. From among the silvery gum wafted a steady refrain of "book-book, book-book," as if to remind me what I was trying to escape. It was a southern boobook owl, Gerry assured me.

I think we must have passed out in a stupor that night, because when I woke with the sun in my face, the wallabies had carried off the bread we had intended to toast over the fire for breakfast. Gerry had slept with the stash under her head—a trick she had learned in India—and so she rolled us an early-morning joint instead. Then we walked up hills and down gullies for a whole day, through the open sclerophyll forest made brilliant with wattle bloom and alive with a myriad of birds. Other than raucous kookaburras and the rainbow lorikeets, I couldn't tell one bird from another. Gerry showed me the bronze-wing pigeon, the fantailed cuckoo, the rose-crowned fruit dove, the golden whistler and a cute little fellow with a red breast and a call like a startled child. A mistletoe bird, she called it.

On that trip I discovered the thing that most recommended Gerry to me as a kindred spirit: she loved musicals. Her mother had owned a collection of soundtrack records, and Gerry knew the words of *South Pacific*, *Oklahoma* and *My Fair Lady*. I was delighted, having spent the last eight years keeping my own passion for the musicals hidden, singing to myself only when I was alone. As we strode through the bush, we took huge pleasure in belting out the lyrics:

I'm gonna wash that man right outta my hair
And send him on his way!

Later on, I tried to broaden her tastes to George Gershwin, Irving Berlin and Cole Porter. Without success. Rodgers and Hammerstein were as retro as Gerry was prepared to go.

There was another magical time, in the summer, when we drove all the way up the north coast to Byron Bay. A scientist friend had gone down to the Antarctic and left me to look after his travel-strained Range Rover. It had a tape deck and an icebox to keep things cool, and it was big enough for us to sleep in. Every day was intensely hot and cloudless blue as we sped along the coast road, with all the windows wound down, marvelling at sun sparkling on the cerulean Pacific as the waves rolled in to the perfectly sculptured coastline.

Linda Ronstadt pumped out of the tape deck:

Soooo goodbye, I'll be leav'n
I see no point in this cry'n 'n' griev'n . . .

We had a week of champagne picnics. The icebox was packed with pork and veal terrine, marinated baby octopus, dolmades, satay prawns, stuffed eggs, leek tart and various cheeses. As well, we carried tomatoes, figs, melon, olives and pesto. I recall us charging full tilt down a dirt side road, throwing clouds of dust, in search of hydroponic straw-berries because they were the perfect accompaniment for the brut rosé we drank as an aperitif on the beach each evening.

Those hydroponic strawberries are seared into my mem-ory: the explosion of astringent sweetness in the mouth, the cricket ball sailing toward us in a perfect arc, the champagne flute in Gerry's hand disintegrating in a shower of tinkling glass and the good-looking bloke who sprinted up the sand dune to retrieve the ball, full of laughing apologies.

He threw the ball back to his mates and flopped into the sand to accept Gerry's offer of a glass of bubbly. She disap-peared into the night with him. A few weeks later he looked Gerry up in Sydney and she dropped everything to go off with him. Next thing I heard she was working in a mining camp in the Kimberleys, in Western Australia. Then she dis-appeared out of my life completely until just a few months ago, when she found my Web site.

Having finished my solitary meal, I pull on a swimsuit and walk down to the lake where Gerry is stretched out on the dock, her arms behind her head, staring up at the rising moon. It is a balmy evening at the very end of summer. The moon glows as the last of the sunset stains the western sky with streaks of red and orange, reflected in the motionless lake.

To my surprise the lake water is silky and buoyant, not sharp and stinging like the sea; a swallowed mouthful tastes faintly of vegetation. Soundlessly I breast-stroke toward the sunset, each arm motion creating a rippling wake of maho-gany and orange. Turning back into the reflection of the risen moon, the water is like mercury before my face, and my shoulders shine in the moonlight as if touched with phosphorescence. The moonlight plays on my flesh as I tread the water to listen to the plaintive call of the loons on the far side of the lake.

Years ago, beside another exquisite lake, in Quebec, I was told this haunting call was the voice of a long-dead Cree warrior still seeking entry to heaven. I feel for a small moment as if I have slipped into heaven. The still night air is pleasantly free of insects when I climb out of the water onto the moonlit dock. Outside the nearest cabin, two very substantial women are having a great time. The sound of beer cans popping and good-natured, raucous laughter floats toward us. They haven't come here for the murder either. Their husbands are out fishing on the lake.

Gerry fetches a bottle of single malt and two glasses. We sit on the dock and talk about my quest to follow Lillian.

"Do you reckon she slept out?" Gerry wants to know.

"Probably. She did have money, though, to buy food."

"Don't fancy her chances." Gerry licks the edge of the paper to seal her cigarette. "A woman on her own, living rough. She'd get raped, sure as apples."

I have often thought what a hazardous business it would have been. The Depression hadn't begun and there were not large encampments of homeless men along the route, although in some ways large transient camps may have provided a greater degree of protection for a woman travelling alone. Lillian would have been at considerable risk. It is little wonder she carried a short length of iron bar concealed in her clothes. Not that it would have served much purpose. Of course, she may have been prepared to trade sex for food and shelter, and this barter may not have been as repugnant to her as my sensibilities imply.

Gerry breaks my reverie. "So we start following her route from here?"

"Right. After she left Vancouver, she headed back to the Telegraph Trail. So, if we aren't completely lost, we're heading for Ashcroft, where the telegraph begins."

"Who cares if we're lost. It's more fun that way."

"We are *not* going to get lost."

"Whatever you say, Cassandra." She stretches out a lean, brown arm for another shot of Scotch. "You point. I drive."

From the neighbouring cabin, more beer cans are popped and shrieks of laughter and affectionate banter assail us: "Gawd, Sylvie, I just love ya to death."

Gerry and I share a complicit smile as we drain our glasses. It is a grand night for female bonding.

Expertly she rolls herself a last cigarette, flicks open a lighter and inhales deeply.

A bit tipsy myself, I reach out to squeeze her free hand.

"What a time we're going to have together on this trip. Thelma and Louise will have nothing on us."

Gerry regards me with her head to one side, eyebrows drawn together. As she blows out the smoke, her face relaxes into a familiar grin, displaying her strong, white teeth.

"Now there's a challenge!"

Birken to Lillooet

In the warming morning air, dragonflies hover and fish leap around us while we frolic in the tepid lake. It would be lovely just to loll about here for the rest of the day, but our trek has barely begun.

Hoisting myself onto the dock, I scan the detailed forestry

map of the area. We are expected this evening at a friend's house near the village of Ashcroft, B.C. Broken lines indicate that the road we are on is a four-wheel-drive track that runs for about seventy kilometres to the town of Lillooet.

Gerry climbs onto the deck and shakes herself like a dog, spattering the map with drops of water.

I suggest to her that we go back to the sealed road and take the marked route to Ashcroft from Pemberton.

She wants none of that.

"Bloody hell, Cassandra, the car is a four-wheel drive. We might as well see what it can do." She takes the map and peers closely at it. "Look here"—her finger traces various faint lines marked "summer only"—"we'd end up at the same place for sure. And it'd be a helluva lot more interesting than that two-lane blacktop." She scrutinizes the map a bit longer, then hands it back to me. "Yeah, that's what we should do. Relax. Let things happen."

Early afternoon, as we are leaving, we make inquiries of our hostess about the condition of the summer-only road going north.

"I wouldn't drive over it. Haven't been over it for years. My husband's driven it a few times." She gives us a doubtful once-over: me rosy-cheeked and grey-haired in baggy jeans and T-shirt, while Gerry is bare long arms and legs, her torso covered by an old school tunic she has tie-dyed. The front of her tousled blond hair is hennaed to a flaming red. "I'd say it all depends on your frame of mind."

On this sunny afternoon at the beginning of the journey, our frame of mind is pretty adventurous.

"We have a four-wheel drive," I say. "Might as well give it a whirl."

She glances at our impressive, brand-new Pathfinder. "Should be okay. You only got a small car."

I am astonished by her observation. This Pathfinder is the biggest car I have ever sat in.

"The passenger gets the worst of it." She fixes me with a warning look.

I realize soon enough that she wasn't talking about the passenger getting a bumpy ride. Vertigo, more like it. Just wide enough for a large vehicle, it is a rocky track, which has been cut into the side of a mountain, just below the snow line, to provide access to the high-tension power lines. On my side, there is a perpendicular drop into the canyon below, with nothing remotely like a guardrail or a protective barrier between me and oblivion, just about thirty centimetres of raw dirt and rock and then empty air. It's a bloody long way down. All my jokes about doing a Thelma and Louise no longer seem so smart. I close my eyes tight on the hairpin turns.

I'm picking up good vibrations . . .

With the Beach Boys full blast on the CD, Gerry's jaw is set tight in concentration. The wraparound Ray-Bans blank out her expression, but she looks to be enjoying herself hugely with the window down and the sun catching the bright red henna in her hair. Just as I remembered, she is a brilliant driver. I allow myself to relax a bit and take in the dramatic vistas.

Looking straight down, I see a flooded canyon, the water tinted teal blue by the fine ash washed into it from the streaks of moraine that pour down the stern, grey face of the mountain like insipid gravy. Vertigo aside, it is a spectacular sight.

"Fucking Jesus!" Gerry yells.

I whip my head away from the view as a small red Jeep comes hurtling around a bend straight at us. The startled driver, no more than a boy, swerves and hits the brakes. The Jeep skids into the mountainside. The driver and his equally young companion tumble out, laughing.

"Are you all right?" I call out.

"Yeah, sure," they boast. "Don't worry about us, Grandma."

"What a pair of dickheads," Gerry mutters, cautiously moving the car around them. If they had slightly misjudged that swerve, we'd be floating in the lake by now. She is stung by their contempt. Furiously silent behind the wheel, she drives extremely slowly, just in case there are any more youngsters out for a spin.

Get around, round, round

I get around . . .

We cross several mountain gorges with rushing streams and miniature waterfalls. Just as the road appears to be coming to an end, it starts to climb, once again looking dangerously precipitous on my side. I realize now what our informant was talking about. If I ever met a road with attitude, this is it.

With relief we finally reach Sefton, about halfway to Lillooet. There is only one road out of the town, and on my map it is marked in black: a real road. It proves to be a slightly better-maintained version of the horror stretch we have just left. We climb and climb right to the top of the mountain, ears popping, then descend in a series of tight switchbacks right to the bottom of the valley. Vertigo gives way to motion sickness. I dare not tell Gerry this; it will do nothing to improve her mood, which hasn't recovered since our close encounter with moronic youth.

Anxiety hovers around us both. We've been two hours on the road to Lillooet without seeing another vehicle. No road signs. We are getting scared. The sun has left the valley and the terrain looks ominous. The realization kicks in that this must be the wrong road.

"Where the bloody hell are we?" Gerry asks.

"We're in Deep Shit," I reply, doing my best to sound like Susan Sarandon's Louise. "Deep Shit, Arkansas."

Gerry can't even manage a smile as she drives on, looking vainly for someplace to turn. Suddenly the road brings us alongside a massive hydro lake and heads directly into a granite mountain.

I see what appears to be a ragged hole punched in the base of the mountain.

"Go," I say, with a jerk of my head in the direction of the mountain.

"Are you sure?"

"Yeah, hit it."

Gerry drives straight through the hole and out into the sun-drenched, barren majesty of the Fraser River canyon.

Two-lane blacktop all the way to Ashcroft.

No worries.

On hearing our car, Peter McAllister comes out into the dusk to welcome us.

"Whatever took you so long?"

I explain how we decided to take the Birken–Sefton–Lillooet road.

He is incredulous. "So it's true. Australians are crazy."

Peter is a retired shipping executive from the United States turned rancher in British Columbia. He is also a passionate conservationist with much in common with my husband, Michael, who was once a career naval officer. They have the same vehement determination to save the planet.

Dinner is waiting, served on the deck of McAllister's farmhouse just as the stars emerge. Coyotes yip and yowl to each other beyond the river flats that Peter has parcelled into fields with picturesque post-and-rail fences. We have sockeye salmon and new potatoes, served with corn picked that morning. I like it so much I finish off the cob Gerry has left uneaten on her plate.

Over dinner I supply a shorthand explanation of our trip.

"We are on a kind of feminist adventure. A cross between *Thelma and Louise* and the *Two Fat Ladies*."

My quip falls flat, since neither Peter nor his wife has seen the famous movie, or the TV program of the two eccentric middle-aged women who ride about the English countryside on a motorbike and cook up marvellous dishes at each place they visit.

"I'd say it was closer to *The Odd Couple*," Gerry murmurs.

She has jokingly mentioned this movie a couple of times since leaving Vancouver. She seems to identify me with the Jack Lemmon character.

I do wish my sinuses were not going berserk.

Presenting a more sober account of our trip, I sketch the story of the woman who walked to Russia and our mission to follow in her footsteps all the way to Siberia. This merely confirms Peter's initial appraisal that Australians must be crazy.

After dinner Peter shows videos he has made of the coastal rain forest of central British Columbia, magnificent and ethereal river valleys where wolves stalk the estuarine tidal flats and families of grizzly bears chew contentedly on the bright sedge grass. All of this area is designated to be logged in the next few years, and some sections have already been roaded. Peter has been ringing alarm bells about this for seven years, pretty well a lone voice until two years ago, when Greenpeace International took it on as its major forest campaign. It was Peter who gave the region its compelling new name, the Great Bear Rainforest. His son's wonderful photographs have given the campaign stunning images.

The grizzly is listed as a vulnerable species in British Columbia, and Peter claims that this awesome creature may well disappear from the province if its rain-forest habitat is any further eroded. In another video, he shows chilling footage of bear carcasses, headless and pawless, left to rot by poachers and trophy hunters.

"People are allowed to hunt grizzly bears in B.C.?" I ask in amazement.

"Sure. It'll cost you up to $18,000 with a registered outfitter," Peter explains, with an exaggerated shrug of his burly shoulders. "Trophy hunting is out of control on the rain coast, and with poaching on top of that, many more than the allowed annual quota of 350 bears are being killed, a lot of them females. This is very remote country. Who is out there to regulate?" He drops the parody of nonchalance and becomes volubly indignant. "In the last six years we have conducted aerial reconnaissance, slogged up rivers and combed the estuaries of the coast and we've never once come across a conservation officer. They don't see the headless carcasses. They don't see the bear blinds."

"Bear blinds?"

"Permanent hides built above salmon spawning streams or near estuarine sedge meadows, where hunters wait for the bears to come and feed." He flips open a ring binder to show us several blinds he photographed within the borders of the Fiordlands Provincial Park. "Completely illegal."

Gerry is deeply affronted. "Don't tell me you can hunt bears in a provincial park?"

"Of course, this is British Columbia." Peter's laugh has a furious edge. "I told the parks branch about the blinds in 1994. As far as I know, they are still there. They said they had no budget to go to the Fiordlands."

Peter believes passionately that what is left of these incomparable coastal river valleys must be protected, or very soon the grizzlies and the rich ecosystems that support them will be lost. In his view it is not enough to put aside the small area of the Khutzeymateen Valley as a grizzly sanctuary; it is way too small to preserve a viable population and is still vulnerable to hunting and poaching.

"Shit, eh," says Gerry enthusiastically. "If those grizzlies are gonna disappear we'd better get in there and take a look at 'em."

"It's right off our route, Gerry."

"Grizzly bears, Cassandra. How can you resist?"

"Because we have to keep focused on Lillian, simple as that."

Gerry's eyebrows knot as she considers this ultimatum.

"How do you know she didn't go there?" she says stubbornly. "Face it, you don't really know how this Lillian person got to connect with the telegraph line in the first place."

Her disappointment is so transparent that I relent and ask Peter to show us a detailed map of the central coast. Sharp-eyed Gerry finds just what she is looking for. In nearly all the inlets along the coast, there are symbols to indicate fish canneries. Asked about them, Peter explains these are all closed now and the abandoned buildings are being reclaimed by the rain forest.

"Don't you see, your Lillian could have got up the coast from Vancouver that way." Gerry's finger traces loops from one cannery to the next, stopping at the settlement of Bella Coola, in the heart of the coastal rain forest. From there, she draws a straight line across to the Cariboo Highway.

I agree that it doesn't seem so far to take a detour to Bella Coola. Just to be sure, I put in a call to Michelle Shaether, an Australian contact at Greenpeace who is the co-ordinator of the campaign in the Great Bear Rainforest and an environmental colleague of my husband's. As luck has it, she is flying in to Bella Coola the day after next.

I arrange to meet her at the Bella Coola airport.

Raven Road

Bella Coola is impossibly remote. Nowadays the best way to get there is to take a ferry up the fabled Inside Passage, a flooded mountain range created by the glacial meltwater of the last ice age. When I made that trip two years ago, the Inside Passage was enveloped in mist, and all I saw was a procession of ghostly, miniature mountains rising sheer from the sea. As the ferry turned into the channel leading to Bella Coola, rays of sun broke through the mist, revealing a white granite bluff along the one side, and on the other the elongated King Island, covered to the waterline with moss-draped rain forest of majestic hemlock, red cedar and Sitka spruce. A pod of orca whales cruised through the channel alongside, creating streamers of silver in their wake before the mist settled back again. Were it not for the fog, I could possibly have seen wolves along the shore in search of a dead dolphin, or even grizzly bears come down to feast on the salmon.

One has to be lucky to see anything much in the perpetually mist-shrouded, sodden landscape of B.C.'s coastal fiord country, where waterfalls gush from every crevice. Even in midsummer, the sun is not seen for days. The central coast gets nearly five hundred centimetres of rain every year, I explain to Gerry as we drive across the Chilcotin Plateau, and the area boasts champion swimmers who practise their strokes while walking to school.

The road we are travelling winds through an endless terrain of stunted lodgepole pines. Mesmerized by the endless spindly trunks, I wonder if Lillian walked through terrain like this. In my mind's eye, I had imagined something much more majestic.

Traditional post-and-rail snake fences zigzag along both sides of the road for the whole length of the forest, some three hundred kilometres.

"Where are the birds?" Gerry wants to know. "Why are there no birds?"

"Maybe they've already gone south. There is always the raven." I point to a big black bird soaring above us, its glossy plumage almost purple against the sky. "He seems to be our sole and constant companion."

"Urrgh. I hate those birds." Gerry gives a shudder.

"You don't say that in these parts. Raven is a cultural hero. He is the one who brought life and order in the world. Nothing could exist without Raven. He is celebrated everywhere on totem poles. Didn't you notice that at the Museum of Anthropology?"

Gerry doesn't respond. She had been less than enthusiastic about my dragging her off to the Museum of Anthropology.

"Anyway," I add brightly, "what is a raven today could just as easily be a wolf tomorrow."

"You don't say."

"Sure. The First Nations believe that Raven has the knowledge of how to become other animals and to speak their languages. It is true. They can mimic the calls of other species, especially wolves. I read that the Kwakiutl people along the coast here offered the afterbirth of male babies to Raven so that when the children grew up they would commune with Raven. I've got a book about all this stuff."

I reach over to rummage in my bag on the back seat.

"Now listen to this," I say, producing the research notebook in which I had rewritten the creation tales of the Pacific Northwest.

In the beginning there was nothing but soft darkness. Raven beat his wings until the darkness packed itself down into solid earth. Soon pale, sickly creatures appeared. They were two-legged, with no feathers, and instead of strong wings they had stick-like arms that waved constantly. Raven felt sorry for them, and plucking a branch from an alder he scattered the leaves on the surface of the sea till fish began to jump. Now that they had fish to eat, the people were very thirsty, so Raven flew to the one spring of fresh water in all the world, guarded by a fierce creature named Ganook. Using all his wiles, Raven tricked Ganook into letting him put his beak into the spring and he drank until he could barely lift himself off the ground. As Raven lifted his head for a last gulp, he saw Ganook coming at him with a huge club. With one tremendous flap of his wings Raven flew clear of Ganook and wobbled across the sky with little streams of water spurting from his beak. These became rivers: first the Nass and the Sitka; then the Taku and the Iskut; lastly the Skeena and the Stikine—all of them as crooked as snakes.

I close the book and turn to Gerry, who is looking fixedly ahead.

"Don't you think that's fascinating?"

"I can't pretend that I do."

As the empty road winds before us, we each become increasingly glum. The endless forest of lodgepole is punctuated by massive clear-cutting operations. We have never seen such great swaths of forest laid bare. I put *My Fair Lady* on the CD to cheer us up.

You'll be sorry
But your tears
Will be too late.

Gerry is amused by the CDs I have brought with me. Her own choice of music is very different. She remembers the words to the musicals, though, and we both sing along, just like the old times. At the top of our voices.

Just you wait!

We settle into silence as Gerry drives on. By late evening we are both depressed and tired and don't know what we are going to do. I had wanted to reserve a cabin for us to stay in before we left, but Gerry wouldn't agree, insisting that I needed to reclaim my sense of adventure.

By now all my sense of adventure has drained away. What must it have been like for Lillian after those long, empty days of trudging when the night enfolded her and the forest went black. Would she have been able to find a hunter's cabin for the night, or would she have lain on the ground cushioned by pine needles and slept, using her boots for a pillow? I would like to talk through my speculations with Gerry, but she seems entirely absorbed in the road ahead.

At last we find a roadside lodge to fill up on gas and make inquiries. Chatting away, the genial owner lets slip that the logging has stunned almost everyone in the Chilcotin.

"It's all because of the beetle," he says.

In the last five years the spruce and pine of British Columbia have become vulnerable to a bug that threatens to destroy the forests. The major forestry companies have reacted by taking out as much of the old growth as they can, before the beetle does. The lodge owner doesn't want to be too critical of the forestry companies but is disturbed.

"Those lodgepole pines don't look like much, but they did take a hundred years to grow. Whatever is going to replace them?"

"I find those pine forests dreadful," Gerry calls over her shoulder as she strides off to the washroom. "They can trash the lot, as far as I care."

Gerry's aggressive outburst surprises me. Her blood sugar level must be low. Lunch was off the agenda and now dinner also seems to be a lost cause.

Before we leave she buys a large bag of lollies to tide her over, and two large packets of potato chips. I am hungry too, but nothing in this fly-blown store can tempt me. I have a list of cabins in the next hundred kilometres and use the road-house phone to ring them all. Every one of them is full.

We drive on to see what turns up. Gerry has a packet of Air Crisps between her seat and mine, and I find myself munching potato chips along with her. My hunger pangs I keep to myself.

After dark we pull into a small fishing resort and rouse

the proprietor. She does not have a cabin free, but the desperation in my voice causes her to take pity. Two fishermen are away for the night, she tells me, and we can sleep on top of their beds in our sleeping bags.

It's a deal. No haggling. Out with my Visa and she gets paid twice.

Gerry is utterly exhausted from the long drive. I fetch some wood and cook up a vegetable curry on the wood stove. I also load myself up with vitamin C and break out my emergency supply of antibiotics. I know this is a very Jack Lemmonish thing to do, but my sinuses are throbbing.

Assessing the smallness of the cabin and my snuffling, Gerry takes her sleeping bag outside to the porch.

Bella Coola

Michelle Shaether is waiting for us when we arrive at the Bella Coola airport.

She is in her early thirties, with long blond hair and long legs: a healthy Australian beauty. She looks tired. The Great Bear Rainforest is a big campaign. Greenpeace has already persuaded quite a few European companies to boycott British Columbia timber products and is running a massive European media campaign. At Bella Coola she has been working closely with members of the Nuxalk Nation, who claim the area on King Island as their traditional land. Like all the First Nations in the region, the Nuxalk are profoundly split on the subject of logging. The elected band council supports the logging because of the promise of jobs, even though the biggest company has just closed up shop in Bella Coola, with the loss of a good many jobs in the town.

In 1995 a group of Nuxalk, including hereditary chiefs, mounted a logging blockade on King Island. When logging was reopened on King Island in 1997 the Nuxalk again blockaded, with support from a coalition of environmental groups. The focus of their rage was the logging in the Ista Valley, sacred to the Nuxalk as the place where the very first woman descended to the world. Chief Quatsinas was arrested at the blockade in 1995 and again in 1997, along with twenty-four others.

Michelle offers to take us to meet this "greenie" chief. Gerry declines, telling Michelle that she has had enough enviro-speak for one day and wants to walk to the hot springs she has seen advertised in the tourist brochure.

At the Nuxalk reserve, Michelle is unsure where exactly Quatsinas lives. She stops at one house and questions the little girl outside.

"Is your daddy home?"

The child hesitates and Michelle repeats the question.

"Well"—the child shuffles her feet and cocks her head sideways to look up at us, "he sleeps over sometimes."

It's the wrong house. Her mother comes to the door and directs us to the trailer with a broken Cadillac alongside.

I recognize Chief Quatsinas from a television program I saw before I left Australia. When we enter the trailer, he is on the phone to someone from the BBC who is researching a program on sustainable forestry, a concept he treats with open derision.

Quatsinas has no time for claims that the logging companies have something to offer his people. They have deserted Bella Coola, he points out. Left people high and dry. I had heard that one company is training young people from the nearby Heiltsuk community. Temporary jobs only, in his view, all for show. The loggers who work along the coast come mainly from Vancouver Island, not local native communities.

"At one time there were sixty-five loggers in our community. Now maybe there are six. Most of our land has been trashed. And what will the Nuxalk be left with?" He spreads his hands to signify nothing. "There is no salmon in a clear-cut, there is nothing to hunt in a clear-cut, I can't engage in my spiritual practices in a clear-cut."

The chief deeply distrusts everything about the Canadian political system and insists that the Nuxalk Nation should stay out of the process to negotiate treaties with the B.C. government that would secure them title to land and monetary compensation. On the other hand, he doesn't trust the legal system and does not advocate an appeal to the courts for the recognition of land rights. Whichever way he looks at it, extinguishment of Native rights is the desired outcome of political and legal process in Canada.

"So what do you think the Nuxalk should do to protect their land?" I ask.

"The best deal for us is to stay outside the court system and the negotiation of treaties and put a stop to the resource extraction on our land."

If I knew him better I would argue about this. Nuxalk territory has already been heavily logged. I am gravely skeptical that his proposal is a viable option, even with European boycotts. I reckon this savvy chief is in a no-win situation.

Michelle's next meeting is with the young activists at the communal house of the Forest Action Network. Several of these kids have suspended prison sentences and one has already done three weeks in jail. In the chaotic living room, they sit in a circle on the floor discussing communal responsibility. Someone has been letting a stray cat into the house. This is against the rules. Only human animals are allowed inside.

"I should not be made to wear a guilt trip because I put the cat out of the house," protests one young woman wearing dreadlocks and a nose ring.

"We shouldn't be so anthropocentric," insists another young woman with a shaved head. "Cats have rights too."

A pale, spindly boy, whose dreadlocked red hair would put Bob Marley to shame, solemnly adds his view. "The cat does make a contribution to the household. She catches the mice."

Consensus is not in the air.

I leave Michelle to it.

There is no museum or tourist information centre that I can locate in Bella Coola, only the office of the Mid-Coast Forest Region, which is full of gorgeous brochures extolling the benefits of sustainable logging. It no longer matters to me that there is no history of the place, because I am sure that Lillian did not come here. When I considered the map back at Ashcroft, I was persuaded that she could possibly have caught a ride on a boat connecting the many fish canneries along the coast, and then cut across to the Telegraph Trail from Bella Coola. Now I am confident she did not. That route is far too circuitous. My strongest sense of Lillian's personality relates to her stubborn single-mindedness in holding to a straight course, in contrast to my companion, who always needs to veer off to the left or right. Faced with the thought of the long drive back across the Chilcotin, I know instinctively that Lillian would not have gone that way.

Another thing I know is that I am not prepared to sleep out among the lodgepole pines, even if that was how Lillian spent her nights. Finding a pay phone at the town's only café, I take advantage of Gerry's absence to book a cabin for our return trip. We'll be there in about six hours I tell the owner.

Inside the café, coffee is terrible and the muffins are the size of a baseball glove. Hostility is palpable. At the adjoining table two burly fellows are talking. Loudly. About logging. About how the rain forest needs to be cut or it becomes degenerate. About the damage environmentalists are doing to overseas markets.

Greenpeace is only in it for the money, they tell each other. "Oh, it's not these hippie kids we got here. They are just being used. It's the boys in Europe who are taking home big change."

I suspect this loud talk is for my benefit. Bella Coola is a very small place, and no doubt I have been observed visiting with the dreadlocks. In no time the conversation shifts pointedly to the matter of clear-cutting and bears.

"Sure those clear-cuts don't look no good at first, but the trees grow back, now don't they?"

"Yeah, yeah. The berries grow first thing. And those grizzlies just love clear-cuts—it's so easy for them to get the berries."

"That so?"

"Yeah, anytime you go out to a clear-cut, you most likely'll see a big grizzly. They love it."

When Gerry returns from her hike, where she failed to find the hot springs or see any bears, I suggest we check this information. We drive out to a clear-cut on the side of a mountain, following a logging road into the valley for about ten kilometres. The devastation stuns us both. It is just raw, bulldozed earth and charred piles of wood. No berries. No bears. The glacial stream running through the valley is muddy from the runoff. A newer clear-cut farther along the road is even more distressing, since it seems like only the cedar has been taken. Great trunks of hemlock and spruce lie smashed on the ground. It costs a huge amount to get these logs out, Michelle had told me, and prices for hemlock and pulpwood are low right now because of the Asian economic meltdown. It is too awful.

We have seen enough of Bella Coola.

On our way out of town we finally encounter bears. At the town dump, six fat black bears nuzzle contentedly among the plastic garbage bags while two Nuxalk men also scavenge among the detritus.

"Never seen a lady so close to bears before," the older man remarks as we clamber out of the Pathfinder. He presents us with a toothless grin.

We are no ladies and, anyway, these bears don't look as if they would do any harm, so greedily are they concentrating on the contents of the garbage. They resemble the stuffed-toy variety much more than fierce man-killers. Black as the glossy ravens with which they share Bella Coola's rubbish, the bears have perky round ears above mild brown eyes and a stumpy, reddish muzzle. For most of the time we watch, their muzzles are stuck in a food container of some kind. The dexterity the bears display as they inspect each bag of garbage is impressive, twisting the lids of mayonnaise jars and squeezing toothpaste tubes. How could you be frightened of an animal with a passion for toothpaste?

"Are there ever any grizzlies here?" Gerry asks.

"Sometimes," the toothless man volunteers. "They chase black bears away."

"Not many." His younger friend corrects. "Grizzlies around town get shot."

When three hours later we arrive at the cabin I had reserved, our host is caught by surprise. He is a good deal younger than either of us and has pulled his long hair into a ponytail. I detect a powerful whiff of marijuana as he steps out the door.

"Oh yeah, the lady from Australia. You didn't take long. Didn't you stop for the sights?"

"There aren't any sights," Gerry snaps at him. "Only trees."

I explain to him that we have been on the lookout for grizzlies.

"How 'bout that," he says dreamily. "We had a young male come around the property only yesterday."

Gerry's interest is suddenly revitalized. "Is it likely to still be about?"

"Nope." He looks grim. "One of my guests got real nervous, so I had to call the conservation officer to come and trap it and move it someplace else."

"So he has taken it, then?"

"Nope. He just went straight out and shot it."

Babine Mountains

At Williams Lake, where the Bella Coola road meets the Cariboo Highway running north, we drink coffee the colour and flavour of sullage water and search the high-resolution map for the old road that ran between the telegraph relay cabins. The map is a crazy paving of logging roads resembling the cracked glaze of an old tile. Not one faint line reveals a purposeful direction. We would get hopelessly lost in there.

Gerry questions the sullen waitress, who tells her to ask the tourist information centre in the next town, which she says is Quinnell. A smile would kill?

"If it's called Quin-nell," Gerry snarls, "why the fuck do you people spell it Ques-nel." She thumps down money for the coffee plus the obligatory fifteen per cent tip and heads for the door.

I knew she should have eaten some breakfast.

At Quesnel I send Gerry to get some food from the supermarket while I interrogate the tourist information office. The woman on duty can't believe that I want to leave the broad sweep of highway with its zooming procession of log trucks and tour buses and long-distance haulers. Even when I attempt to explain about the woman who walked to Russia by following the telegraph line, she remains nonplussed. She has not the first notion about the Telegraph Trail. Never heard of it.

Two-lane blacktop remains our only sensible, if boring, option.

A century ago the Cariboo Highway wasn't so dull. In the days of the gold rush, when men from every walk of life and every corner of the globe descended on the Fraser Valley, the modes of transport were very idiosyncratic indeed. Best of all were the camels imported by a local entrepreneur in the belief they would withstand the harsh, dry conditions. The camels were hopeless because their feet were not suited to the rocky trails and because they caused havoc among the mules, which bolted if they caught even a whiff of camel, scattering and smashing the supplies. Horses, too, were afraid of the ungainly beasts. They would rear in terror, throwing their riders and overturning coaches. When they were turned loose, the camels survived for a while in a pocket of sagebrush, that tough, silvery shrub that thrives in desert-like conditions and exudes a wonderful smell.

We have some sagebush on the dashboard of the Pathfinder that Gerry picked when we left McAllister's ranch. Days later, it still fills the car with an astringent, peppery aroma.

The Yellowhead Highway to Hazelton is dull indeed. We veer off on a side road that leads to the Babine Mountains Provincial Park to go for a hike, following what appears to be an old logging road for many kilometres.

"Better put on bright orange jackets in case some bozo mistakes us for bear," Gerry quips. She sounds tart. "Don't suppose these people clear-cut their provincial parks, though God knows they might. If it moves, shoot it. If it grows, cut it down."

More than tart.

Once we enter the park boundaries, the road rapidly deteriorates to a track of slush and potholes. No logging here. It's dense forest. The sun does not penetrate the tall pines. This is more the kind of terrain I had imagined for Lillian's trek. Coming toward us, very slowly, is the ranger in his truck. He stops, obviously concerned: what are two women with foreign accents doing all the way in here?

"We wanna go for a walk," Gerry announces. "That possible?"

He ponders this for a while, as if such a request is unusual for a ranger in a provincial park. Somewhat hesitantly, he points us in the direction of one trail. Straight up the nearest mountain.

I am not altogether sure about this.

"Your body could do with a big sweat," Gerry insists, with an edge of belligerence in her tone.

She takes off up the trail ahead of me. Having stripped off her shirt, she bounds up the trail in her sports bra and floral miniskirt, sandals on her feet. I plod behind in my hiker's boots, carrying a change of T-shirt and socks, as well as a polar fleece jacket. I know about hypothermia in this changeable weather. What is not commonly understood, I have tried to tell Gerry, is that most people succumb to hypothermia when the temperature is between zero and ten degrees Celsius.

Can it be that she has not been listening? _____

It is a very steep haul and I am sweating profusely, much more than a body should sweat. Gerry is completely out of view. Several of the trees show signs of bear scratches, and the trail has lots of brilliant pink splotches of regurgitated berry pips where the bears have been browsing. Berries are in great abundance here: raspberries, elderberries and salmon-berries grow all along the side of the trail, while deeper in the forest the understory is a mass of bright red bunchberry.

Do I fight back or play dead? What precaution refers to which type of bear? The only bear-like creature I am famil-iar with is the dopey koala, permanently zonked on eucalyp-tus leaves. The most damage a koala can do is to piss on you if you unwittingly stand under its tree.

As I trudge around each hairpin turn of the trail, I look fruitlessly for the sunshine that will signal the end. Each turn brings me yet another hairpin, with a steeper incline than the last. While I am still below the treeline, my nose starts to bleed. I have never had a nosebleed in my life before. When I call out, my voice seems to be absorbed by the for-est. I change my sweat-drenched clothes, gather a handful of raspberries, put on my jacket and sit down on a fallen tree to wait.

"With black bears you stand your ground," I tell myself. "For grizzly bears you roll into a ball and play dead." I cannot envision myself standing toe to toe with a bear. Mentally I rehearse rolling into a ball.

Here is my first real intimation about just how difficult that trek must have been for Lillian. This country is comparatively easy; we are not even into the high country of the Skeena Mountains and I am whacked. I reason with myself that I obviously have some virus, while in the back of my mind the germ of suspicion begins to form that Lillian never did walk the Telegraph Trail, that her story is apocryphal.

After quite a long time, Gerry comes striding down the trail. She looks at me with something close to contempt.

"Couldn't make it, huh? Nothing to see up there anyway, just more trees."

I show her my bloody T-shirt.

She shrugs. "Probably blowing your nose too hard." Then she relents a little. "I wouldn't have expected you to get even this far. It got so steep it nearly did me in."

"I thought you might be waiting up there for me," I croak faintly.

"Naaa. I wouldn't do that."

The walk down takes close to two hours. At the trailhead we find the ranger sitting in his truck looking worried.

"I felt real bad," he says. "It's a hell of a climb. I should not have suggested it."

Gerry swaggers slightly, hands on hips. "Easy peasy."

She makes coffee on the portable fuel stove and breaks out food from her supermarket supplies. "Get this," she reads off the side of the packet. "Each one of these has only sixty calories. That's the stuff for us, wouldn't you say, Cassandra?"

She hands me a slab of puffed rice with chocolate coating that I assume is going to be our dinner. Taking a bite, I find it has the taste and consistency of sugared polystyrene. I guess I can eat this crap if I have to. Once in a while.

On the blacktop once again, Gerry lets loose with a diatribe against the dankness and density of the pine forest and the way no sunlight penetrates the canopy.

"I can't pretend that I like Canadian forest," she pronounces.

"Have no fear, Geraldine," I murmur. "You are not pretending."

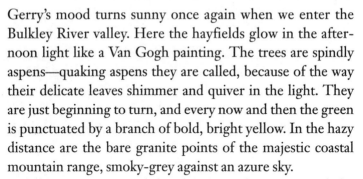

Gerry's mood turns sunny once again when we enter the Bulkley River valley. Here the hayfields glow in the afternoon light like a Van Gogh painting. The trees are spindly aspens—quaking aspens they are called, because of the way their delicate leaves shimmer and quiver in the light. They are just beginning to turn, and every now and then the green is punctuated by a branch of bold, bright yellow. In the hazy distance are the bare granite points of the majestic coastal mountain range, smoky-grey against an azure sky.

The river is named for the man who supervised the abortive Collins Overland Telegraph. Charles Bulkley had two crews working on the line to cut a trail across vast mountains and glacial valleys for nearly three thousand kilometres into the raw wilderness of the Skeena Mountains, as far as Teslin Lake. An army of one thousand men had worked on the project, with five hundred axemen clearing the trail in preparation for the wire-laying crews. When the news came through that the transatlantic cable had made the project redundant, they simply upped and left. Half a century later, backwoodsmen around Hazelton could still find wires hanging from huge blocks and insulators fastened to the trees. Most of the movable material was taken by the Gitksan and Tsimshian people, who made good use of it, turning the insulators into cups and making nails out of the wire. From the discarded cables, the Gitksan constructed a large suspension bridge across the river canyon.

At the small town of Smithers we stop at the Bulkley Valley Museum, which is largely devoted to the construction of the Canadian Pacific Railway, but it does have a folio of photographs of the telegraph line as it was in 1911. The trail would not have been much different fifteen years later, the curator tells me.

There are photos of the first and third cabins on the line. They are set among clearings less than a quarter of a hectare in size, where the rough ground is covered in tree stumps and fireweed until it hits a towering wall of straight-trunked pine trees that all but obliterate the mountains in the far distance. The cabins were constructed from the felled logs, laid horizontal in a double thickness and chinked with mud, while the roof was made from rough-hewn boards secured by wire. They do not appear to be much larger than one room, with a rudimentary porch and an elevated lookout tower, possibly for fire spotting. Very prudent, since a wildfire in a place like this would be utterly terrifying. The tower would be equally useful for storing food out of reach of the animals. Bears can climb, all right, but that flimsy structure could not support their weight. Clearly visible in front of the cabins is the telegraph line, strung along bare pine trunks. In one photograph a pack train of maybe twenty fully laden horses and mules stands outside the cabin. It interests me that there are so many animals in the one place, yet there appears to be only one man with them.

I ask the curator what she thinks this pack train would be.

"Oh, that would be the one from Hazelton to provision the telegraph line once a year."

"Only once a year?"

"This was very remote country, you know. Relay men were expected to be pretty well self-sufficient by trapping and fishing."

"God, what a lonely life."

"Could be. Could be. They were always sending messages to one another. Playing chess. Swapping recipes." She pauses and considers the matter more thoroughly. "I tell you, I have never heard any stories of anyone going mad. Men worked on the telegraph line for many years at a stretch. Must have liked their own company, eh?"

What most interests me is a photograph of the Telegraph Trail cut through a pine forest even more dense than the one we have just left, the telegraph wire hooked between trees with their lower trunks stripped bare. Beneath the wire the trail is cleared about two metres on each side, so it would have been relatively easy for Lillian to follow, except that tree trunks are strewn higgledy-piggledy across the trail, lying where they have been felled. Moreover, where our trail snaked up the mountain in a series of S-bends, the trail in this picture climbs straight up to the summit.

Gerry wanders over from where she has been studying mining equipment from the last century and peers over my shoulder.

"You fancy walking hundreds of kilometres through that?" I ask, glancing up at her.

She makes an exaggerated grimace. "Not me, mate. Not on your life."

Could Lillian really have walked that telegraph line all the way to Dawson?

Other than the photos and the copy of published memoirs that I have already seen, the museum has nothing on the telegraph. There is the diary and reports of a long-serving member of the provincial police that I eagerly scan, looking for clues, but sadly he left the Hazelton force ten years earlier than the period I am interested in. The museum has no other material relating to the provincial police.

If Lillian came through the Bulkley Valley, as she is said to have done in the fall of 1927, and again early in the summer of 1928, there is no evidence of it. Not a scrap.

Cruising alongside the Bulkley River beyond Smithers, we catch sight of salmon making their determined way to their spawning grounds against the torrent of a small waterfall, and stop to marvel at their astonishing acrobatics. It is not clear what kind of salmon these are—probably steelhead or coho. They are mighty big fish, about a metre in length, with metallic blue backs and silver sides, shooting several metres in the air, propelled by the tail, their battered bodies flashing.

Along the river, signs spell out the regulations for fishing for salmon, with stern warnings not to take any coho or sockeye. The wild salmon stocks are badly depleted from logging, dam building and other human depredations. Along the Pacific coast, fear and loathing have gripped the once voracious commercial fishery, and boat owners faced with strict quotas fling angry accusations in every direction but their own. Sport fishing, which is a form of religious observance in these parts, is beset with restrictions. We hear the fishermen grumbling everywhere we go.

Where there are salmon, there are fishing cabins where we can get accommodation.

At Hazelton we head down the rough dirt road that runs through the Gitksan village of Kispiox. Comparing my hand-drawn map of the Telegraph Trail with the road map, I decide that somewhere between here and the Skeena River must have been the spot where Lillian emerged out of the bush to confound Bill Blackstock at number two cabin in September 1927. Since the cabin had been built on the site of a Tsimshian village, it might still be here. Almost certainly there would be a track of some kind, since the relay cabins continued to be used by trappers and fishermen long after the operators were finally withdrawn in the 1950s.

The cabin we find is not from the telegraph but it sure is rustic, part of a basic fishing lodge set in a meadow beside the Kispiox River. It has two sleeping platforms, each with a mattress and pillow, a wood stove and a pile of logs. Gerry sets to with the axe and soon has a roaring blaze in the stove, while I do my best to explain why I want to try to find the place where Bill Blackstock first saw Lillian.

"What's so special about that?" Gerry demands.

"Don't you see? It is the first time anyone really registers what she is trying to do."

"Must have thought all his Sundays had come at once," she says with a lewd grin. "A woman emerging out of the bush. Couldn't believe his eyes, I'll betcha."

Too true. For those men living in isolation for months on end without seeing anyone, fantasies about women appearing out of nowhere were probably an occupational hazard.

Mind you, this woman, gaunt from malnutrition and her clothing in shreds, would hardly have been anyone's sexual fantasy. Still, sex is something I must take into account.

Thanks to Gerry's fire, the temperature within the cabin has risen above thirty degrees. I am so bushed that I fall asleep almost immediately, zipped into my nylon cocoon.

I wake to the sound of my own hoarse snore. My sleeping bag is completely soaked through with sweat. I can tell by her breathing that Gerry is awake, though she gives no indication. Waves of her silent fury radiate through the cabin. Mortified that my snoring has kept her awake, I grab my pillow and stumble out into the delicious chill of the night. In the back seat of the car I toss feverishly for a night of hallucinatory, violent dreams.

Early next morning I add massive doses of vitamin C and garlic to the antibiotics in an attempt to knock over whatever is playing havoc with my sinuses. As Gerry is still hunkered down inside her sleeping bag, I walk over to the main lodge to pay for our cabin and to find out if the taciturn proprietor knows anything about the Telegraph Trail.

It has become very important to me to locate some tangible evidence that Lillian did in fact walk through here. Everyone hereabouts knows about the Telegraph Trail, he tells me, since Hazelton was once almost totally dependent on it, as the supplier of the pack train that made annual food drops along the trail. An old forestry map tacked on his wall has the dotted line of the telegraph clearly visible. It goes right by here. I rest a knuckle at the place on the map.

He shakes his head firmly and slowly.

"Never find it now." He is adamant. "Not on your life."

Salmon Glacier

The Pathfinder seems to be the only vehicle on the Cassiar Highway heading into the subarctic fall. In just two days the colour has changed dramatically, with the simmering banks of yellow aspens now dominating the patchwork of trees across the plateau, while on higher ground the mountains are glowing rusty red and burgundy from the wild roses. The high peaks of the Cassiar mountain range display their first dusting of snow.

"Damned if I know why these people go on about this being a lousy road," Gerry remarks, cruising at 130 kilometres an hour.

Most car rental companies expressly forbid their cars to be driven on the Cassiar, even those with four-wheel drive. I had the devil's own job getting a car that could be taken on such a road, and then only because I agreed to pay an outrageous insurance premium.

"A piece of piss," Gerry proclaims. She is already bored and wants to turn off onto the rough dirt road pointing to New Aiyanish on the Nass River.

"Not a good idea," I say firmly. "First up, it is not on our route map."

She raises her eyebrows to indicate exasperation.

"And second"—here I think my reasoning will carry more weight—"New Aiyanish is in the heart of the Nisga'a Nation. I doubt those Indians are going to welcome us as representatives of white-fella decency and generosity."

Gerry is ill at ease in First Nation settlements, as I am. It is not the uniform look of poverty in the dilapidated trailers and battered Cadillacs that disturbs us. It is our sense that this is a world to which we are not attuned. We perceive hostility even if it is not there. And there is almost certainly going to be hostility from the Nisga'a.

Some two thousand square kilometres around the Nass has been granted to the Nisga'a in the first of a series of treaties between British Columbia and its First Nations. British Columbia hums with outrage about it.

It is hard to see why people are so worked up. True, the Nisga'a will get a payment of $190 million over fifteen years, but only $14 million of that will come from the British Columbia government—less than one-tenth of one per cent of British Columbia's annual budget, as the government press release emphasizes—the rest is from federal reserves. Anyway, no one else really wants the remote Nass Valley; only the Nisga'a live there. They have been granted less than ten per cent of the territory they claim, and the forestry companies that are remorselessly stripping the area have the right to continue logging, with no royalty to the Nisga'a for another five years.

Nope. We don't want to find ourselves face to face with people who have been given such a raw deal.

Gerry remains skeptical at my explanation and slows the Pathfinder so she can take a look at the map. "Hello," she says with sudden new enthusiasm, "the Salmon Glacier, that's the trick!"

"Gerry! It's way off our route." I hear the tone of an exasperated schoolteacher in my voice.

"Ya gotta learn to take risks, Cassandra. Do the unexpected." She flashes me her toothy grin. "No need to get your knickers in a twist. We'll find your Russian woman."

"Belorussian," I correct. "I told you, she was from Belorussia."

Heading for the glacier we get stuck behind a modest recreational vehicle—RV for short—with the legend JESUS LOVES COWBOYS proudly emblazoned in big, bold letters on the rear end. Gerry, who has the keener sight of younger eyes, draws my attention to much less significant lettering that has added AND COWGIRLS TOO. She scoots past at the first opportunity, but very soon has caught up with a much larger RV lumbering along at about thirty kilometres an hour. This one's rear end proclaims OUR JUDICIAL DICTATORSHIP, CRIME AND INDUSTRY ARE DEADLY AND MUST GO.

RVs are the best reason there could be for keeping off highways. Consumerism on wheels, they are enormous gas guzzlers equipped with every imaginable gadget, so Ma and Pa Kettle can travel the continent without leaving behind their cable TV, dishwasher, microwave, heated toilet seat, automatic ice cubes, AstroTurf and the rest of life's necessities. They can put a man in orbit for a year with less technological support than the average RV has. Most of them are so gigantic that they tow their cars. It is infuriating to get caught behind one of these things. Pa Kettle always drives ever so slowly for fear of having to brake hard, which might cause the roast dinner to come flying out of the oven. They are impossible to pass on a single-lane road—which is why they all have messages painted on their rear end.

Proselytizing to a captive audience.

As we drive across the perfunctory border from Stewart, British Columbia, into Hyder, Alaska, the Portland Canal is smothered in a dense cloud just beginning to lift. The dreary scene of maritime industry is transformed into something mystical, as elements of dead tree stumps and log rafts and tugboats and cranes emerge out of the swirls of cloud. By the time we are well into Alaska, the clouds have dissipated sufficiently for us to glimpse the towering Tongass rain forest, where gigantic spruce trees, dripping with lichen, run up the sides of mountains above us. A rutted, slush-filled road carries us along the river toward the Salmon Glacier.

"Bear," announces Gerry, applying the brakes. Sure enough, a very large bear, presumably male, ambles out of the bush to cross the road in front of our car.

"He is definitely a grizzly," I explain excitedly. "He's got a brown coat and the distinctive hump."

"I can see that for myself, Dr. Know-it-all."

The huge beast gives us not a momentary glance as he pads down to the riverbed that, we now realize, is boiling with spawning salmon. We stop to watch him, absorbed as he is in fishing. Grizzly bears must be short-sighted, as this one seems to be concentrating on feeling for the fish in the silt-laden water. Triumphantly he rears up on his back legs with one big beauty speared on his mighty claws. More like kitchen knives than claws. As the salmon twitches in his monstrous paw, the bear tears off its head and skin, then tosses it aside, going down on all fours again to feel about for another. After a couple of partly eaten salmon, he is satiated and lumbers up the bank on the far side of the river, looking as amiable as a gigantic, shaggy dog.

We are beside ourselves with pleasure at being witness to this.

Within the next kilometre another grizzly appears near the road, heading just as purposefully for the river. This time we are less hesitant in moving to the bank to watch. To our astonished delight there are already three other bears midstream; a mother and two cubs are splashing about, in play rather than serious eating. There is no reason for them to be hungry.

Hundreds of salmon drift listlessly in the water. They don't look appetizing. A physical transformation takes place in the long struggle to spawn that changes their silvery pinkness to a brilliant crimson and gives the males a humpback and a grotesque elongated snout. Having already spawned, the fish shudder and die before our eyes. Spent carcasses float belly up in the current or catch along the riverbanks. Cawing ravens peck at what the bears discard. Both sides of the river are littered with dead salmon, and the smell makes us pinch our nostrils.

The road leaves the river and climbs higher into the mountains, again enveloped in clouds. The spectacle of the Salmon Glacier threatens to elude us, but no, an opening between two banks of cloud reveals a flow of ice between the multiple peaks of the mountains into one stupendous frozen river sweeping toward us. Dark streaks of churned-up moraine indelibly mark its inexorable forward movement, and the ridged and rucked-up surface of the glacier is coated with centuries of dust. The myriad clefts reveal the compressed ice to be the colour of pure aquamarine.

We push onward, even though the road has deteriorated to a narrow rocky track, determined to get as close as possible. When the road comes to an end, Gerry presses ahead on foot in an attempt to get photos on the rugged surface. It is too cold for me; the wind off the glacier penetrates to the bone marrow. Even from this distance I can hear the ice popping and cracking as it imperceptibly moves forward. Standing in the lee of the car, I am content to watch Gerry as she scrambles across the rucked surface of the ice in candy-striped jeans belted tightly at the waist. She has obviously lost a lot of weight recently. The jeans are far too loose on her.

She returns exhilarated.

"Stand over there and I'll take your photo against the backdrop of the glacier," she commands.

When the shutter clicks, I reach out to take the camera to photograph her. She jerks it away.

"Naa. I'm too old and ugly. No way you'll get a photograph of me."

I am dismayed at this. Gerry is an attractive woman.

"You're not old, for God's sake. You look terrific."

She turns her back and climbs into the cabin of the Pathfinder.

Driving back to the Canadian side, I am delighted to find a health-food store in the town of Stewart, where I buy some organic dried fruit and a big bottle of multivitamins. Gerry adds licorice and a packet of herbal laxatives. Outside the store there is a stall selling fresh organic vegetables. Tomatoes. Zucchinis. Lettuces. Beans. Carrots. I buy them all, even the mean-looking, spotty apples and some small green chilies.

As the long twilight begins, we stop beside the road in a sheltered spot for dinner, which we cook on our portable stove: egg noodles with a mix of the chopped vegetables and all of the chilies. At the last minute Gerry decides to add some chili paste for additional flavour. The effect of this on my throat is indescribable. My eyes swim with tears while hunger struggles to compete with pain. Gerry bolts hers down, without a blink, even more hungry than me.

"Hope it's not too hot for you?"

I weakly shake my head and persist with the noodles, gasping intermittently. That much chili is guaranteed to give me the burning shits. How can Gerry possibly want laxatives when she eats chili like that?

She suddenly grabs my arm and points ahead quite a way where a large black bear has lumbered on to the road. Immediately sensing our presence, he turns tail and disappears back into the woods.

"Holy shit. The woods are full of bears." Gerry is both awed and frightened as she flings the food back into the car and dives into the front seat. "Let's get out of here."

The car is in motion by the time I have shut my door.

"That does it," she announces. "You're not getting me on any more hikes with all those bears about."

"Come on, Gerry," I remonstrate. "There have been bears about all the time. It didn't worry you before."

"That is as may be. You want to go for a walk, go by yourself."

We drive on in silence as the empty road winds ahead and darkness begins to envelop the brooding Jack pine that carpets the surrounding hills. Anxiously I watch the speedometer climb steadily to 140 kilometres an hour.

"We're going too fast."

Gerry slows to 120 with a derisive snort. "Can't have you chewing your fingers all the way, Cassandra. But then you're sure to find something else to get anxious about."

I put the soundtrack of *The Singing Detective* on and sing softly to myself:

On my cayoose
Let me wander over yonder . . .

A sense of dread has begun to descend as surely as the darkening gloom. Can it be that Gerry and I are not the right travel companions for each other?

Telegraph Creek

"The trouble with this country," Gerry expostulates, "is that it is so fucking empty."

We are heading for Telegraph Creek, through country of sun-drenched glory. Since leaving the glacier, we have driven over a hundred kilometres, past several population centres marked on the map, but have seen nothing at all, just the occasional rest stop beside the road.

"Are you disappointed?" I can't imagine anyone being disappointed with this stupendous landscape.

"Naaa. It's fantastic to look at. Just no people. I expected there to be . . . you know, towns."

I point out there is a town marked on the map at Bob Quin Lake. We will stop there, I tell Gerry, because it is the one place where the route of the Telegraph Trail connects with the highway, and so is sure to have something about the trail, maybe evidence of Lillian. It was called Echo Lake when Lillian came through, I explain, and it has since been renamed after one of the longest-serving relay men. No doubt he will have left some memorabilia we can look at. Gerry gives scant appearance of listening, although she does perk up at the mention of a town.

We are both stunned with disappointment to find that Bob Quin Lake is just an empty rest stop beside a stretch of water. There is no sign of the telegraph, no interpretative plaques, nothing. Casting my eyes to the mountains that loom on either side of the lake, I find it almost beyond conception that Lillian walked across country from Hazelton to here. It would have been utterly impossible without the cleared trail of the telegraph, and even then the stretch between Hazelton and Telegraph Creek was known to the linemen as the most dangerous and difficult.

Quite apart from formidable mountains, the fast-flowing rivers of the Nass, the Iskut and the Stikine have cut deep canyons twenty metres wide and almost that deep, through which boisterous water rushes at great speed. We saw one such canyon near Hazelton, traversed by a beautiful suspension bridge. In 1928 the only way across these canyons was a kind of aerial tramway made from twined strands of the strongest telegraph wire, from which a platform of stout board, one and a half metres long, was suspended via a small pulley wheel and secured by a clevis. Once catapulted into the air, the weight of the body on the board would send it speeding to the other side. Whole pack trains that made the annual supply run from Hazelton would use these contraptions, unless of course the wire snapped or the clevis pulled out, as was known to happen, plunging the hapless passenger into the torrent below. Smaller streams and tributaries, no less dangerous when swollen with spring melt or heavy rain, were crossed by means of fallen tree trunks, slippery as glass.

Wolf packs were no longer prevalent by the 1920s, but there were still wolves in this wilderness, as well as cougars and lynxes. And of course the bears, especially the big grizzlies. Lillian travelled alone and carried no gun to fend off an attack. That she survived without being drowned or mauled, and without any broken bones, is surely miraculous.

She may have avoided the big carnivores, but she would have been terribly persecuted by the stinging, biting bugs that have been known to drive hardened bushmen out of their minds. The infamy of these biting insects in the far Northwest is why I chose to travel at the very end of summer.

As well as mosquitoes the size of zeppelins, the region is notorious for swarms of tiny blackflies that slice off minuscule pieces of flesh in order to get blood. They dispense an anticoagulant that causes the blood to flow freely. The mosquito, on the other hand, sucks the victim's blood through a long proboscis. Only the female mosquitoes bite, and they are so keen on the job that they have adapted so they can breathe through their abdomen to keep their mouthparts free for feeding. There is another little monster that goes by the name of no-see-um. Naturalists estimate that defenceless animals in the subarctic can lose a pint of blood a day to these winged vampires.

Lillian was pretty defenceless against these insects. When she arrived at cabin number eight, hungry and exhausted and severely sunburned, her face and arms were swollen out of all proportion from bites. The two relay men at cabin eight, Jim Christie and Charlie Jantz, had heard over the wire that she was coming but had not expected her so soon. Shocked at Lillian's condition, they persuaded her to rest up in Christie's cabin while he bunked down with Jantz. Her clothes were in shreds and she was so undernourished that in their opinion it would have been impossible for her to move on. Lillian would not listen to sense; after three days she was off again on her trek through the Skeena Mountains. Charlie Jantz, the smaller of the two men, remodelled a pair of his trousers to fit her and also gave her a couple of good shirts, a felt hat and a pair of stout boots, which she could just manage to wear over two thick pairs of socks.

It was on the way to Echo Lake, where Gerry and I have paused for coffee, that tragedy struck.

Jim Christie walked with Lillian over the summit of the Nass toward the next cabin. He had wired ahead to Scotty

Ogilvie, at Echo Lake, who agreed to come out to meet them, even though it had been raining for days and the rivers and creeks were all in flood. He never made it. Christie found his body the next day, caught among a tangle of uprooted cottonwoods in the raging Ningunsaw River where the bank had given way. He had fallen into the maelstrom and broken his neck.

If Christie or any of the other men of the telegraph resented this obsessed woman who had exposed their colleague to fatal misfortune, it is not apparent in their various memoirs, where Lillian is remembered warmly. Even Cyril Toohey, the relieving relay man who came to bury Ogilvie and escort Lillian to the cabin at Echo Lake, had no hard feelings toward her. Nor did any of the linemen who assembled at the lake to bury their comrade. They all showed great generosity, giving her instruction in bush skills. One of the linemen, Tommy Hankin, gave her his valuable black-and-white lead dog, Bruno, to carry her pack.

Hankin gave Lillian careful instructions on how to secure the pack and told her that she must not let the dog run free between the lake and the Iskut River, which was a trapping area. Perhaps she didn't understand. When Moose McKay came out to meet Lillian at the Iskut River, he saw woman and dog reach the riverbank, and observed that the dog took a drink of water, then keeled over dead. He instantly recognized the symptoms of poisoning. The dog had eaten a bait left for wolverine in the vicinity.

I have a copy of a faded photograph from this time, taken when all the men gathered at this very spot for the funeral of their colleague. Lillian is wearing Jantz's striped shirt, cut-down breeches and felt hat, her face and neck covered by a large kerchief worn under the hat. Bruno, laden with a pack, stands obediently between her and Tommy Hankin, just outside the log cabin.

No sign of any of this now.

Dease Lake, two hundred kilometres farther north, is our first real town. It has a supermarket and a liquor store.

"I want to go to a café," Gerry announces. "See some other human beings for a change."

There are several cafés, all much of a muchness.

"Whichever one we settle for, the coffee will be awful," I observe unhelpfully.

Gerry rounds on me. "Jesus, you give me the shits. You're so negative. Everywhere we stop you say the coffee will be terrible."

Me negative? Who is calling the kettle black here? Another low blood-sugar attack, I presume.

"Come off it, Gerry," I say, giving her a mock punch in the arm to keep it lighthearted, "it always *is* terrible. That's why we have a portable stove and a coffee pot to make our own."

So as not to argue any further, I steer her into the town's biggest café, where the coffee is the usual swill, but where they do have a soup-and-sandwich deal for lunch. A marvellous Canadian tradition, these soup-and-sandwich deals. The hearty soup is usually homemade and the sandwiches are huge.

"Just the coffee for me," Gerry says, as I order soup and sandwich.

Since her outburst at the glacier, I am beginning to see myself through her eyes. Old—if forty-plus is old, then fifty-plus is decrepit—and fat, certainly. Ugly as well, I guess, as a necessary condition of the first two. It is a discomforting insight. I am reminded of Gerry's account of the women at the airport in Florida. She went on and on about the size of the women in shorts waiting for their flights. "Gross" and "disgusting" were the words she kept using.

Gross. Disgusting. I roll these words around in my head.

I refuse to think like that. My body needs proper nutrition and that's all there is to it.

When my hefty order arrives, I grow cunning.

"I can't possibly eat all of this. How about I have the sandwich and you have the soup."

Gerry accepts and eats hungrily while I push unkind thoughts out of my head.

Our waitress is personable and talkative, a rarity in Canadian hospitality, where natural reticence can seem like rudeness. She wants to know where we are headed. When Gerry reveals the destination as Telegraph Creek, she is genuinely alarmed.

"Oh my. You're going to drive all that way on that terrible road, eh?"

We nod enthusiastically.

"There's nothing there, you know. No people. No shops. Nothing."

"Sounds good to me," says Gerry, head down over her soup. There is no accounting for what food does to improve her frame of mind.

The waitress remains unhappy with our choice.

"You be real careful, eh?"

We promise that we shall be. Real careful.

The gravel road to Telegraph Creek is just as treacherous as we were warned. Much of its 112 kilometres is a series of precipitous switchbacks. The road climbs into mountains the colour of a darkening bruise, where planes of mauve rock are discoloured with smudges of golden dogbane and the dark olive of the stunted Jack pine. The blue waves of the coastal mountains are in the distance, their snow-covered tips flashing in the sun. After a few dizzying hours, the road descends into the steep-walled canyon of the mighty Stikine River. Wild and unnavigable, this river rips along at such speed you can almost see it slicing through the rock walls of volcanic lava beds on either side. The famous naturalist John Muir saw the Stikine Canyon in 1879 and declared it to be "a Yosemite one hundred miles long." He was not exaggerating.

We stop at a spectacular point where the canyons of the Tahltan and Stikine Rivers meet in a cauldron of churning water. On the wall of the Stikine, glassy spokes of smoky purple with red oxide flashings radiate out from the ochre heart of a massive obsidian deposit, like some huge Modernist sculpture. At the base of the rock, the churning water has thrown up a broad bank of pebbles, forcing the river through a small opening where the local Tahltan have constructed fish traps. Across the road is a Tahltan fish camp with several brightly painted wooden shacks decorated with moose antlers. We go over and ask permission to take a photo of the rock face.

An old man preparing fish tells us proudly, "That is the Tahltan eagle, sacred to our people."

There is no mistaking his open friendliness, and he has no objection to Gerry's camera. Moreover, he offers to sell us some freshly caught steelhead salmon. I agree with alacrity.

Salmon straight out of the water. What a treat.

There are more Tahltan reserves to pass through before we make a steep descent into Telegraph Creek: a cluster of houses perched tentatively on the bank between the rushing river and the bruised rock bluff that towers behind. As we enter, it is apparent that this is largely a ghost town, cut in two sections by the tumbling creek from which it takes its name and terraced into three levels by a series of lichen-encrusted, drystone walls. Abandoned pickup trucks lie rusting on their sides here and there, while most of the ramshackle log and frame houses are completely derelict, with roofs collapsed in on themselves and window frames hanging askew, threatening to topple into the river below. One house has literally slid off its foundations onto a house on the level beneath. Given time, all these teetering relics will descend into the raging Stikine, to be deposited along its banks and gravel beds like so much river debris.

During our descent, my eye is caught by a series of printed exhortations emblazoned on one decrepit building. THE LORD SAYS TO KEEP THE JUDGMENT AND DO JUSTICE, the roof shouts at us. We had seen the exact same slogan painted on a building in Bella Coola. Maybe religious mania is a feature of all isolated British Columbia towns. I hope it is not widespread.

It is quickly apparent that we need have no worry about any human influence being widespread in Telegraph Creek. There is only one permanent resident, the Royal Canadian Mounted Police officer who lives in a newly painted white frame house displaying a cascade of petunias, lobelia and sweet peas from its window boxes. A complex of three frame buildings on the river make up the Riversong Lodge and Café.

Our lodging is two big sunny rooms and a kitchen in the

most imposing of these buildings, the original headquarters of the Hudson's Bay Company, which opened up this wild corner to Europeans in the 1860s in order to trade with the Tahltans. Since the mid-1970s, trade has been run by Dan Pakula and his family, although they don't actually live in town. Dan's daughter Pearl, a lively, open-faced young woman in a long Indian skirt and ankle bracelets, has shut the café and is waiting for us to arrive. Now that summer is over, we are the only guests. They'll close up next week.

Gerry doesn't object as I cut the salmon into several steaks to pan-fry for dinner. We still have fresh lettuce and tomatoes, and the obliging Pearl has provided us with the additional treat of freshly baked sourdough bread. As the fish is cooking, I make us a couple of potent vodka tonics, chilled with the ice cubes thoughtfully left in the fridge.

The feast is served on a picnic table perched at the edge of the bank, where we watch the clay-coloured river surge by. Telegraph Creek is ours alone. Gerry looks relaxed and happy. She likes it here, despite there being no people.

We clink our glasses and agree that Telegraph Creek was worth the ride.

Things will be all right, after all.

Glenora

Outside our lodging, a group of robust young men with a raft are preparing for a long haul down the Stikine to Wrangell, Alaska. It will take about a week, they tell us, as they load up supplies. Wistfully Gerry says she wishes she could go too. The young men do not respond.

This is testosterone territory; there is no place for her.

I can see she really does want to go with them. She always wants to do what the macho men do, yet she wants to be a womanly woman too. I suspect this continuing conflict makes her unhappy a lot of the time.

Disappointed in their lack of interest, she squats down beside the Mountie's dog, which has quickly become her unshakeable companion, and rubs her cheek against his neck. "Let's go for a long walk, eh, boy."

From the car she takes a bottle of water and a bag of raw almonds. Dog and woman bound eagerly up the creek bed toward the cliffs that loom over the river. Even though there is not much water in the creek, it is rushing down the hill at great speed. If this were after the snowmelt, the creek would be a torrent and turn the river into a raging maelstrom.

I don't mind being excluded, since it leaves me free to explore this ghost of a town to see what I can unearth about Lillian's time here. I am disconcerted to find no museum, no history society, not even an information centre.

Pearl Pakula, who is baking sensational-smelling wild-berry pies for the rafters, doesn't know much about the town history, but she can confirm that the author of the religious exhortations on the derelict building was indeed the same religious nutter from Bella Coola. He did not linger long and has now moved on to yet another isolated outpost. As I walk about the town I can see why his proselytizing was of no avail. The soul of the Tahltans was long ago secured for God by the indomitable Christian Missionary Society of the Church of England. They are responsible for St. Mary's, a beautiful brown-stained wooden church with a tall, shingled steeple on the riverbank. St. Mary's is well maintained and obviously home to regular church services, part of the far-flung diocese of the Yukon that has serviced the towns of the telegraph line since 1897. The two glass windows on either side of the altar carry the Tahltan totems of Raven and Bear, as does the striking red-and-black banner above the altar that proclaims Mary as Virgin of the Tahltans.

The houses of Telegraph Creek, however derelict, are still very pretty. Not all are log cabins—indeed, most are made from milled timber, painted bright colours with high, pitched, shingle roofs. These are substantial houses that speak of a once prosperous community; their gardens are a riot of rose bushes and lilac run wild among the glorious elderberry trees, heavily laden with big scarlet bunches. Despite their sorry appearance, the houses exude an air of decayed homeyness, a sense of waiting for habitation to be taken up again where it was left off.

As I feared, there is absolutely nothing in Telegraph Creek to yield a clue that Lillian visited here in 1928. There is no longer any evidence of the telegraph, even though the trail is still marked on topographical maps of the area. While I was able to find some evidence of Lillian's trek between here and Hazelton, I have nothing at all for the 370-kilometre trek from Telegraph Creek to Atlin, although I know she arrived in Atlin in August.

It is a sore disappointment that Telegraph Creek has no secrets to share.

At the British Columbia Archives, I did get a pretty fair idea about the rigours of the terrain between here and Atlin from an account of the Yukon Field Force expedition, which walked the Telegraph Trail in 1898. Five women were included in the force—four nurses and a woman reporter—and they hated every moment of it. Nurse Powell gave this graphic description of the trail:

> From mountain to swamp and bogs—bogs in whose cold, damp mossy depths we would sink to our knees and under which the ice still remains; swamps where we trampled down bushes and shrubs to make a footing for ourselves, and where the mules stuck many times. . . . Through deep forest we went where the trail was narrow and the branches of the trees threatened our eyes or tore our veils disastrously, through tracts of burnt and blackened country, in some places ashes still hot from recent burnings, and the dust rising in choking clouds under our feet; through forests of windfallen upturned trees whose gnarled roots and tangled branches made insecure and often painful footing; over jagged rocks where slipping would be dangerous we went trampling leaping springing and climbing, a strain only the strongest and most sinewy woman could bear. . . .

Nurse Powell and her companions made about twenty kilometres a day, whereas Lillian, dangerously alone and travelling light, covered the distance at about twice that speed. She also moved much faster than Guy Lawrence and his father, who took the trail in 1899 carrying all their heavy supplies of food, plus shovels, pickaxes, sluice cradles and more.

The Lawrences had come from England to make their fortune and wound up in Telegraph Creek, like the tens of thousands of gold seekers heading for the Klondike who saw the trail cut by the abandoned Collins Overland Telegraph to Teslin Lake as a shortcut to the Klondike. They were offloaded by the thousand at the wild and makeshift town of Wrangell, Alaska, and transported in flat-bottomed boats up the Stikine to be deposited at Glenora, about twenty kilometres down the Stikine from Telegraph Creek.

When Guy Lawrence and his father arrived in the summer of 1898, he estimated there were about five thousand stampeders at Glenora in makeshift dwellings that often incorporated materials left over from the abandoned telegraph. With no adequate sanitation or drainage, it was a thoroughly disgusting cesspit.

In faraway places like London or New York, the line on the map from Telegraph Creek to Teslin Lake had been enthusiastically taken for a wagon road. The reality proved more daunting than most could contemplate. While many lingered at Glenora for months in indecisive disappointment, the Lawrences decided to hit the trail on shank's mare, taking their chances walking the trail in the spring of 1899, to steal a march on their fellow fortune hunters.

They had an unspeakably dreadful experience.

Much of the trail was cut through the waterlogged muskeg, into which a man could sink up to his knees. Muskeg is beloved by mosquitoes that Lawrence thought sounded like a million telephone wires singing. The dreadful things came in huge swarms, only kept at bay by continuously burning green brush. Lawrence and his dad endured the chest pains and rasping breath of respiratory problems in preference to the savagery of mosquito attacks. They did finally get through to Teslin Lake, but plenty of others were not so lucky. Lawrence describes taking shelter from the intolerable cold in a derelict cabin, only to find a frozen corpse in each bunk. These men had holed up in the cabin to wait out the winter, subsisting on a steady diet of salt pork and beans. By the time they had died, the slightest scratch had begun to fester, old wounds reopened, bones no longer supported their weight, and teeth loosened and then fell out.

Scurvy. The great killer of the gold rush.

As the stampede continued, the trail became littered with discarded equipment, as well as dead men and their pack dogs.

The ravens and wolves had a wonderful time.

Once the telegraph line to Atlin was completed in 1901, the old trail was improved, with relay cabins established across the Stikine Plateau, at the Sheslay, the Nahlin and the Nakina Rivers, each of which was traversed by an improvised aerial tramway. While it was not quite as demanding as the country south of Telegraph Creek, the relay stations were much farther apart and more dependent on assistance from the local Tahltan. Because the linemen spent the summer months hunting and trapping, there were refuge cabins along the line, equipped with small stoves and stocked with basic provisions.

Guy Lawrence became one of the very first linemen on this stretch of the telegraph, serving at various relay stations between 1902 and 1915. Isolated though it was, Lawrence reported he never heard of anyone cracking under the strain of loneliness. Hunting accidents, frostbite, hypothermia and wild forest fires took a toll, but what caused most suffering to linemen, as Lawrence recalled, was their own cooking. In time, many became highly competent cooks, especially of cakes and pies, and would eagerly exchange recipes over the wire. They ran a competition for whose recipe could produce the best two-decker cake. Along with rum, sugar was a big-ticket item for the pack train.

Lillian would certainly have been heartily replenished with carbohydrates at every cabin along the way, and no doubt departed each with a cache of dried moose meat and baked goods. Keeping up her supply of carbohydrates and making sure she was properly clothed was the best the relay men could do for this woman who would never pay attention to reason.

"We listened on the line and were able to follow her progress from cabin to cabin, and we all wished her the best of luck," remembered Cyril Toohey, the relay man who had escorted Lillian at Echo Lake.

Gerry finds me crestfallen at the lack of information in Telegraph Creek when she emerges from her walk. She suggests a trip to Glenora, where I may yet find something of what I am looking for and she might find some company.

Glenora is clearly marked as a settlement on the map, but what we find is nothing at all, only a trail alongside the racing Stikine that leads to an empty Tahltan fish camp. No sign of life except for the ubiquitous ravens. It takes a big feat of imagination to realize that this small area of flatland was once a tent city for thousands, with makeshift houses, shops and saloons. Looking about us, we can detect only a dirt track leading farther into the woods.

Clambering back into our Pathfinder, we follow the track, mud spitting off our wheels.

"Not a road for the faint of heart," I observe uneasily, glancing sideways.

Gerry has that determined set to her jaw as she shifts into the lowest gear. The bog holes have become more numerous, and more mud spurts onto the windshield. There is no place at all to turn around. I take heart that the woods are very attractive: white-trunked aspens, grown tall and spindly in their struggle for the sun, are bent over by the weight of their sodden foliage, creating a leafy bower for us to negotiate our way through. Now that the rain has ceased, everything is bathed in dappled light. At the edge of the track are bushes of glossy white and red berries, while the understory is a carpet of golden willow shrubs. Finally we come to a tributary track that, to our astonishment, leads through a pine and spruce forest to a log house set amid a voluptuous garden of vegetables and flowers.

Gerry stops the car and we walk toward the house, where we are met by a determined little dog who darts around trying to keep us stationary with his furious barks. The dog's owner comes out to quiet his pet.

"Is this a Tahltan bear dog?" I have heard about these tiny but utterly fearless dogs that would contain a grizzly until the Tahltan hunters came to finish him off.

"Nice thought," the man says with a welcoming grin. "Bear dogs are now extinct, I'm pretty sure. They interbred with other dogs. The Tahltan did not realize they were losing the breed until it was too late. He is a good bear alarm, though," he adds, opening the door to invite us into the house. "He always lets us know when one is around."

For all the dog's fearlessness, our host takes little chances with bears. As we enter, he points to mothballs hanging around the cabin.

"Bears hate the smell of mothballs," he explains, as he draws our attention to an infrared screen by the door that will detect anything larger than his dog.

"Surely a bear couldn't get through this." Gerry looks hopefully at the solid log door.

"Oh yes, he could. Easy as pie once he got it into his head that the house could be his lunch box. So far so good, though."

Rick and his wife, Barb, belong to that wave of hippie homesteaders who came into the country in the seventies. They were able to buy some two hectares of this wild territory from the provincial government twenty-five years ago. At first they lived in a makeshift cabin while they tamed the bush for their garden plot, cut the forest, milled the timber for their house and kept a wary eye out for the bears.

Their house is wonderful: two hexagons joined by a light-filled sewing room. The unlined log walls are chinked with moss, and each room has a different kind of wood on the floor and surfaces, milled from the spruce, pine and aspen of the surrounding forest. There is a solar panel in the roof, but not much more suggests the intrusion of modernity.

Over a cup of tea they talk about their life here.

"We were so naive when we arrived," Barb recalls fondly. "Fancy coming into the country without even a gun."

"And you have one now?" Gerry really wants to know about this.

"You bet." Rick gives a deep-throated laugh. "We've had to shoot two or three bears, but, touch wood"—he looks around to acknowledge that every surface of their kitchen is timber—"we've never had any real trouble."

Every year Rick shoots a moose for meat; otherwise, he trades vegetables and produce with the Tahltan for the sockeye and steelhead salmon they catch in fish traps and cure in the smokehouses we saw along the river's edge at Glenora. He and Barb have raised two kids in this wild isolation, schooled by themselves, now both at university. Only on one occasion has the isolation been a problem.

"Our daughter had a burst appendix one winter. That really scared us," Barb allows. "The only transport was a dogsled to Telegraph Creek. Then we had to radio to get a small plane to come and take her to Smithers. Took us forty-eight hours." She puts her hands to her rosy cheeks and closes her eyes momentarily, flustered and pained to remember that distant terror.

"After that I put in the radio phone." Rick points to a set-up rather like a radio booth in the kitchen corner.

No more medical emergencies. Both are a picture of health.

In their garden they have a big vegetable plot still fruitful with the last of the season's crop. Barb picks us bush tomatoes and pulls some carrots. As we are leaving, she presents us with a bunch of fresh basil.

"Dinner can be the rest of the steelhead with tomato and basil salad," I burble happily as we drive away. "With a bit of luck we might cadge some home-made bread from Pearl."

Gerry nods absently, her mind on something else. "I don't know how they could live like that, with all those trees around the house. I'd go crazy. I'd have to take an axe to 'em."

Is it possible to be tree-phobic? Can there be such a thing as arboriaphobia?

Dan Pakula is waiting by our lodging to present the bill.

Dan, too, is part of a movement of hippie homesteaders who just squatted on the land around Glenora in pursuit of an alternative lifestyle. He is from my era, having come of age in the heady sixties, and he came into this country in the early 1970s. In the mood of the times, he and a group of other settlers established a communal store in Telegraph Creek. Now he is the only one left. He makes the best of the summer months outfitting fishermen and rafters and providing food and accommodation to tourists who come to experience the true West Coast wilderness, including his very expensive boat trip down the Stikine to Wrangell. Things are fairly tough for him for all that. Affable though he is, he is keen to be paid in case he is not around when we leave in the morning.

When we quiz him about the Telegraph Trail, which I fondly imagined I might be able to follow to Atlin, he is quick to disabuse us of the notion.

The telegraph was closed in 1942, he explains. For some time the trail was kept clear, but it's now heavily overgrown and very hard to get at. Dan walked the trail once, many years ago, when he was a much younger man. From here to Atlin took him two weeks.

"An absolute bitch," he says with a shudder. "Worst country I ever walked. Be lucky to do fifteen k in a day."

No one has managed to construct a road of any kind across the route of the telegraph to Atlin, even after a hundred years. The only road to Atlin, Dan shows us, is a circuitous loop route, long and tedious by the look of it. In contrast, the line of the Telegraph Trail runs straight across the plateau to Atlin.

Just like those obsessed gold seekers a century ago, I have read into that line on the map my own needs and desires.

In order to get to Atlin, we cannot follow the route that Lillian took. Instead we must drive all the way around the Stikine Plateau. This involves a retreat back to Dease Lake, up the Cassiar Highway to the Yukon and westward along the Alaska Highway until we reach a solitary dirt road that runs back toward the Stikine and terminates at Atlin.

The Al-Can

In a steady stream the RVs on the Alaska Highway are all heading the other way, home to Clarksville, Tennessee, or Cedar Rapids, Iowa. The only competition going our way comes from Greyhound and the long-distance commercial road haulers. To fit the mood, Gerry has installed one of her own CDs of good trucking music.

Momma hated diesel real bad
I guess it has som'thun to do with dad . . .

The Southern Yukon is magnificent country of rough-cut purple hills, where the aspen are a quivering lemon-yellow and the wild roses are turning to burgundy. The aspen leaves tremble and shimmer like a shower of precious coins. Along the road the blood-red seed pods of the fireweed and the crimson swamp-currant bushes compete for spectacle with the burnished gold of creeping dogbane.

Gerry pulls into a rest area beside an exquisite turquoise lake so we can make coffee. As the coffee percolates, she produces a packet of spicy BBQ shapes.

I groan. "Come on, Gerry, let's make some real food."

"Wazamatterwisis?" Her mouth is crammed full of salty triangles.

"You know perfectly well that stuff is crap, Geraldine. Bodies need proper food."

"*You* need food, Cassandra. Let's face it, food is all you ever think about."

Now it's my turn to lash out. "I'm not the one who has to shovel shit in my gob every few minutes. I don't spend all day eating potato chips and lollies and smoking cigarettes."

She looks stricken and I curb my tongue.

"I'm sorry, I don't remember you like this. You always loved food."

"And I got *fat*!" She spits out the last, loathsome word.

"Don't be so idiotic."

"You can say idiotic, Cassandra, but fat is fat."

"Like me, you mean?"

Gerry turns away to pour herself a cup of coffee, which she takes down to the lake. I can tell by the set of her shoulders that she is miserable. That makes two of us. Hot tears prick behind my eyes.

Some feminist adventure.

As Gerry shows no desire to be back on the highway, I bring out the food and chop up some vegetables that I toss into boiling water with some packets of instant Japanese noodles. Normally I loathe instant noodles, but since Gerry bought a swag of the stuff, I hope that these may tempt her. When I call she comes willingly enough, accepting her bowl of noodles with an awkward half smile. She adds a big dollop of chili paste and devours the noodles noisily, beads of sweat breaking out on her cheeks and forehead.

"Hot stuff." She wipes the back of her hand across her face. "That's great!"

As if nothing has happened between us, she cheerfully dismantles the Tranjia stove, packs up the food box and locks them into the trunk of the car.

"Righto," she says, flipping the keys in the air and catching them with her other hand, "time to hit the road, Momma."

I resolve to put the whole ugly incident out of my mind. When all is said and done, she was a good friend.

Once upon a time.

After dark we reach Teslin Lake, where we stop for a break. Gerry slumps across the wheel, clearly exhausted.

"Why don't you let me drive?" I ask. "You can't possibly drive to Atlin tonight."

"I'm the driver, Cassandra," she snaps, jerking her head up. "That is the deal. I do the driving. You give the lectures."

"Okay. We stay here tonight." I am not going to argue about this.

The motel beside the lake is full. Alongside the highway is another desolate-looking establishment. In the stale-smelling, poorly lit bar we negotiate a room and agree to take a twin-bedded double. It is the last they have, and it gives the word "tacky" a new resonance. The room is clean enough, but every surface has cigarette burns and the bedcovers are threadbare. There is a TV. Gerry and I climb onto our respective beds to watch.

Gerry takes the remote and runs through 121 channels that transmit nothing but static and snow, with occasional sound. The only channel properly visible is for the hearing impaired, with everything subtitled using word-recognition software. We watch a program called *It's a Strange Universe*, which features interviews with people who have been having visitations from reptilian aliens from outer space. This is serious. It's not being played for laughs, even though the subtitles are full of ludicrous mistakes.

A pinched-faced man explains how he got tips on the horses—in code—and when he had figured out the code he made heaps. Now, unaccountably, the reptilian aliens have deserted him and he is losing again. Another interviewee, a faux blonde in her mid-forties, tells of having wild sex with reptilian extraterrestrials. "They can do anything a normal man can do and more," she tells the young reporter breathlessly.

Indeed. A strange universe.

The gravel road to Atlin, though we were warned about its condition, fails to challenge Gerry. At the very first opportunity she diverts down a narrow dirt road where a crudely painted sign promises smoked salmon.

"Here's the go, Cassandra, more tucker for you!" she exclaims gleefully as the Pathfinder jolts and bucks over the potholes.

The signs lure us on for another fifteen kilometres to a log cabin where we find a couple in their late twenties who have dropped out of the hustle and bustle to fetch up with this precarious existence, smoking and selling salmon caught by the local Tlingit people. The cabin has an unfinished feel, and the woman, while friendly enough, gives off an air of low-level desperation. We are their first customers today, she tells us. And their last, I'm confident. In sympathy I buy a big hunk of smoked chinook salmon.

The appalling road comes to an end at a clearing beside an overgrown stream, where Gerry thinks she can detect a walking trail leading into the woods. It doesn't look safe to me. No signposts.

"I don't think we should do this," I say firmly. "I once tried walking in the woods without a trail and it got very scary."

"Really?" Gerry's sarcasm is all too evident. "And whenever could that have been?"

With not so much as a backward glance she is off at a striding pace, oblivious to the bears that once so alarmed her, leaving me to follow, should I choose. Hurt by her contempt, I do attempt to follow, although, after pushing my way into the dank spruce forest for ten minutes, I retreat.

Blinking in the sunlight as I re-enter the clearing, I find myself face to face with a wild-looking man of about my own age, with unkempt hair and beard, brandishing a very long knife.

I stare in wide-eyed shock. I have no idea what action to take when threatened with a knife. Rolling into a ball isn't going to help.

"It's grand out here, eh?" he says affably.

I nod, heart pounding, while my eyes dart around for an avenue of escape.

"They say the cress is best farther down the creek," he continues. "You've been down there, eh?"

I focus on my questioner and see that he is holding a serrated breadknife.

"Sorry?"

"Cress. In the creek. I'm going to cut some to go with my fish. You come from England, eh?"

"Australia," I say, feeling the sweat running down the back of my neck.

"I'll be. Always wanted to go to Australia. It's great fishing down there, eh?" He wanders off toward the creek to get his greens.

"Good watercress too," I call after him with a relieved smile.

Looking about me with new eyes, I see that weeds grow to a giant size here. The dandelions are at least a metre high, with flower heads about ten centimetres across, while the red clover sprouts huge pink powder puffs. Electric blue dragon-flies hover around them. The whole environment seems to be charged with magic.

This must be how it felt to Dorothy when she entered the Emerald City.

By the time Gerry reappears, I am sitting with Hank—for that is his name—on the step of his camper van, eating a watercress sandwich made with delicious, freshly baked bread.

"Glad I didn't have to send out a search party," I call out as she comes toward us. What a sight she presents with her tangled vermilion hair, skirt tucked up into her knickers and a T-shirt that proclaims ALL MEN ARE BASTARDS.

Hank springs to his feet, bug-eyed.

"Gidday, mate," she says when I introduce them.

Gerry is the same height as Hank, who beams at her with unabashed delight and offers a sandwich, which is accepted without a flicker. Between hungry mouthfuls Gerry details where the best fishing spots can be found in outback Australia. Her special knowledge on the subject of fishing comes from her father, who is a fishing fanatic. His great disappointment was that he never had a son, so Gerry was the substitute. When she was a child he would take her on a fishing trip to the Murray River every Christmas holiday.

"The best part was fattening up the maggots he used for bait to catch Murray cod. Great creamy things he kept in sawdust." She gives a momentary shudder, while her face lights up with delight. This is a story that gives her a special bond with Hank, who is on a fishing holiday with his son.

He just can't take his eyes off her.

Hank walks with us back to the Pathfinder and stands awkwardly beside the driver's window as Gerry buckles her seat belt. Just as the engine starts to purr, he reaches through the window and puts a large brown hand on her arm. "You come fishing with me, eh? Tomorrow morning at Atlin Lake."

Taku Country

Atlin belongs to that part of the vast Northwest that was the last to be infiltrated by white men. The Taku River Tlingit, who are the traditional owners, call the seventy-kilometre lake A'Tlen, meaning "great water." The first known white man to see A'Tlen's glory was Michael Byrne, a miner who had been hired to scout the territory for the Collins Telegraph in 1867. There is some evidence that during the 1880s, Russians from Alaska travelled up the Taku River: Tlingit children had Russian names and the river chiefs spoke some Russian. Long-abandoned mine workings suggest that a few lone prospectors made it as far as Atlin following the Cassiar gold rush in the 1870s. However, the region was not properly explored until 1892, when Narcisse Gauvreau and a team of surveyors mapped the area of the plateau between the Stikine River and the southern tip of A'Tlen.

It was the 1898 Klondike rush that spawned the settlement of Atlin, when word of a secondary strike there spread like wildfire. Obsessed stampeders heading for the Klondike on the Telegraph Trail—people like Guy Lawrence and his father—saw this as a less hazardous option than trying to navigate up the Yukon in makeshift boats and diverting to the south end of Atlin Lake. Others, who had braved the rigours of the steep and treacherous Chilkoot Trail over the coast mountains from Alaska, broke ranks and headed to the western edge of the lake. In summer boat owners had a lucrative business ferrying these wannabe miners across to Atlin. In winter they sledded across the ice, stumbling, snow-blind and frostbitten into the makeshift camps at the lake's edge. When the rush was at its height, during the winter of 1898–99, the mercury regularly plunged to below minus forty degrees.

By the end of 1899 many thousands of men had arrived in Atlin, and even a few remarkable women. Martha Watson tagged along with her gold-struck husband, shepherding their four children—including a two-year-old toddler—over the terrible summit of the Chilkoot and across the frozen lake to Atlin. In the case of German immigrant Helen Lupecke, gold fever struck her rather than her husband, with Helen abandoning husband Johann and their children in Minnesota to light out for the Yukon. After struggling alone over the Chilkoot to Atlin, she established a thriving business of a much-needed laundry and bathhouse, while her sober family stayed on in Minnesota.

Our first view of Atlin is a heart-stopper.

"Will you just look at that!" Gerry exclaims, applying the brakes.

The tension between us, which has been building to the intensity of the atmospheric pressure when a tropical storm is about to break, starts to dissipate as we survey the panorama opened out in front of us: an elongated glacial lake with Ming-blue water, enclosed by bold mountains, deeply scoured by streaks of moraine and pockmarked with dazzling glaciers. It is the kind of awesome spectacle that would send romantic poets into reveries about the sublime.

Around the pretty little town there are quite a few gold-rush buildings, restored as part of a heritage project. Anything over fifty years is heritage in these parts. As most of

Atlin was burnt to the ground in 1914, many of the heritage buildings have been trucked in from the nearby ghost town of Discovery, the site of the original strike. One of the most attractive is now the liquor store, a tiny wooden house painted rusty red, with a stand of massed larkspurs the intense blue of the lake at the doorway and window boxes cascading lobelia, pansies and petunias. Another picturesque building with a mass of flowers in the window boxes is the museum of the Atlin Historical Society.

At the sight of this building my heart lifts. I mentally note to make a beeline there first thing in the morning.

To my delight, the museum has a photograph of Lillian on display, taken on the day she arrived in town.

I study the picture carefully: a slight young woman still dressed in Charlie Jantz's clothing, now quite ragged, with the patched trousers rolled to the knee, her legs covered with thick socks. A felt hat is pulled down to her dark eyes and a stained kerchief hangs down to protect her neck and ears. The overlarge shirt is secured by twine, while her double-breasted jacket is too small. It must have once belonged to a child. Over one arm she carries an empty canvas bag. Thin and fatigued, but otherwise not the worse for wear, she looks away from the camera, a bit distracted. Anxious, perhaps. The photo puts me in mind of Greta Garbo in the movie *Ninotchka*.

Diane Smith, the indefatigable volunteer archivist of the historical society, is keen to talk to me about Lillian Alling, but she can't tell me much about my enigmatic quarry. Marie Murphy took the photo when Lillian stumbled out of the bush onto the Murphy place, just south of Atlin, late in August 1928. No one else paid her much attention. Back then, folks were all too busy with the harsh demands of their own frontier life to be distracted by a woman attempting the impossible. The documentary evidence about her is scant indeed. Marie Murphy, who kept a diary every day of her life, has made no entry about this ragged, half-starved creature who appeared out of the blue.

Such a lack of curiosity is a historian's heartbreak.

Stories about her sprang up many years later. Tall stories. When Edward Hoagland was in Atlin some thirty-three years ago, he was told by two old-timers that Lillian stayed on in Atlin cooking for the miners. They remembered seeing her going down to the icy lake to wash her clothes.

"She did no such thing," Diane Smith sternly tells me. "Any more than she carried the stuffed hide of her husky companion, as they also said." As far as Diane can ascertain, Atlin did not delay Lillian longer than it took her to purchase some food and a new pair of shoes.

"So she still had money, then?" I wonder to myself how much money and where she might have kept it.

"I guess so. I don't imagine they were giving boots away."

The shoes in the photo do not look worn out. If they were the pair that Charlie Jantz had given her, they would have been a poor fit. It is bad enough to contemplate Lillian walking that arduous trail plagued by insects, heat and floods without the additional anguish of ill-fitting shoes.

Diane tells me that Lillian continued along the Telegraph Trail to Whitehorse, where she booked into the Regina Hotel.

So she did have money.

She shows me a copy of the entry recording this fact in the *Whitehorse Star* of 31 August. That is about all she can say.

Stymied in my search for information about Lillian and with time on my hands, I consider what else the museum has to offer. Another arresting photograph is of a darkly handsome man with a prominent moustache wearing formal European clothes, complete with tie, waistcoat and homburg. He stands with one hand on his hip and the other holding the branch of a spruce tree, looking defiantly at the camera.

This is Jige, a. k. a. Taku Jack, chief of the Taku Tlingit from 1894 till 1926.

I have encountered this fellow before. His granddaughter, Elizabeth Nyman, is a Tlingit elder in the town. From her book of the stories of the Taku Tlingit, I had learned that Taku Jack was of the wolf clan. In Hoagland's *Notes from the Century Before*, Taku Jack rates mention as a legendary guide in the early part of the century, when this barely touched region was attracting aristocrats from Europe and wealthy game hunters from the eastern seaboard. These people wanted the very best guide, and Taku Jack was their man. Guy Lawrence describes him as a big man in Atlin around 1900, much respected by the white community. Yet another account of the early days in Atlin tells me that this intelligent, handsome and fearless chief was given a position in Atlin awarded to no other Indian, while the women of Atlin permitted his wife to clean their homes.

Much as Atlin old-timers liked to boast about their respect for Taku Jack, it never extended to providing education for his children. As the pictures in the museum make clear, the Tlingit were not permitted to attend the Atlin school. The only time any education was provided for them was in 1907, when a Catholic missionary set up a rudimentary school within the Tlingit village. The school lasted only until 1910, when the missionary was transferred to Dawson City. The children of Taku Jack and other Tlingit youngsters were forced to endure the indignity (and worse) of residential schools determined to obliterate native culture. His daughter Antonia Jack recalled the residential school she attended, run by vengeful nuns, where she was given only thin porridge to eat and was forced to make her own clothes and to work in the scullery. It is a commonplace, shameful story.

Taku Jack and his people voluntarily sent their children to residential schools because they wanted them to get an education, even though it was likely they would spend more time in drudgery than learning. Antonia Jack in turn sent her children to residential school, despite her own awful experiences. When the youngest child left for school, Antonia found the loss intolerable. She looked and looked at the little shoes her daughter Jenny had left near the door until she couldn't bear it any more. She and her husband went to beg the principal to let her child into the Atlin school.

"We had to beg hard—for what should have been our right," she writes, "but we did get Jenny back."

There is no doubt that Taku Jack liked Europeans, and he chose to dress and act like one of them. He appreciated the economic advantages that mining and hunting gave his people, who could work for wages in the summer and return to hunting and fishing in the winter. Never for one moment did he think that the white men owned the place. In 1915 he was confounded when approached by the McKenna-McBride Royal Commission, which had been appointed by the provincial government to look into the status of aboriginal people. Those Atlin townsfolk who were said to be so respectful of Taku Jack had petitioned the commission to have the Tlingit village moved eight kilometres out of town. The Indians were unhealthy, they complained; many of them were dying of tuberculosis and it was bad for the rest of the town. The commissioners wanted Taku Jack to indicate which land should be made a reserve.

"You got no land to give me," Taku Jack told the commission. "If you give us people a piece of land, we are not free. This is my country and I want to keep it."

Quitting the museum, I stroll around Atlin's few streets. The Tlingit village is still where it always was, on land originally set aside for the natives by the Catholic Church. Three years ago, when I made my first visit to this exquisite place, there were vacant lots growing knee-high fireweed and edible brambles, as well as derelict cabins with collapsed tarpaper roofs colonized by briar roses. Gone now. Cleaned up for the centenary or to make way for the stylish, architect-designed houses that are springing up all around the place. Rich Americans own most of these. If you have your own airplane, Atlin is a very desirable summer location, given that the unsurfaced road severely restricts tourist access to its heart-stopping views.

A little way out of town is the graveyard, always a fascination for a storyteller like me. Judging from the tombstones, those gold seekers that survived the rigours of the journey and didn't succumb to frostbite, scurvy or pneumonia lived to a ripe old age in Atlin. The infamous influenza epidemic of 1919 carried off a few, but otherwise frontier misadventure seems the most likely reason to depart this lovely place before one's fourscore years were up. Here, too, I find the archetypal American tragedy: a sixteen-year-old boy mistaken for a bear and shot by his father in 1940. There are several victims of this kind of misadventure. Variations on this classic American theme can be found almost every day in the newspapers now that the hunting season has started. Only yesterday, a man in the Rockies attempting to unload his rifle shot his son in the head after sitting him on the hood of the car to keep him safe.

From the cemetery I take a trail along the ridge that has been cut through stands of white-trunked aspen, pretty as the lid of a chocolate box. The valley floor has wide splashes of glowing yellow, scarred by the bare heaps of tailings from the worked-over creek beds.

The men who flooded into Atlin in 1899 initially worked the gravel bed of these gold-bearing creeks with shovel and sluice box, but it soon became apparent that the real pay dirt was deeper in the bedrock than shovels could reach. Mule-driven hydraulic scrapers were created to gouge out a flume over six metres long and four metres deep. When this technology proved inadequate, massive dredges were put to work. One dredge had ninety-six buckets, each of which could gouge out a cubic metre once the clay-cemented gravel had been loosened by drills or by blasting with dynamite charges. The Guggenheim family of New York had the biggest claim and a huge steam shovel. The boilers that drove the shovel required six cords of wood a day to fire the boiler. Hence the golden vista of secondary growth in the valley, where once the pine forest grew.

Within a decade, gold mining had turned all of Atlin's creeks into a dreadful mess. Today they are no longer recognizable as creeks; rather, threads of sluggish water meander through the piles of tailings discarded by the dredges and mechanical sluices. There has been no attempt at reclamation, since gold might yet be hidden in those ugly humps of rock and gravel.

I am puzzled by the absence of birds. Not even the raven can be seen. A lone squirrel watches me boldly for a moment before scampering away. Nothing else moves or peeps. I have seen so little wildlife since leaving Telegraph Creek. The woods appear to be empty, yet I know they are teeming with hidden life.

And dangerous.

The idea hits me again like a sudden thunderclap: how did Lillian avoid attack by wild animals? She was carrying food that would have attracted the bears and she would have been defenceless against a wolf. Maybe the bears and the wolves, satiated by the summer salmon and lulled into finer feeling by the beauty of the fall, were not interested in this emaciated and obsessed woman.

For all the disfigurement of the creeks below, this is a very lovely walk. As the afternoon sunshine catches the aspen leaves, I am presented with a shimmering spectacle of colour from intense lemon yellow through sienna to tangerine. Beneath the iridescent aspen, the tall stalks of fireweed have finally exhausted their magenta flowers and turned a brilliant blood-red.

In the soft glory of Atlin, I understand how Lillian managed to keep going. Such natural beauty has an extraordinary power to regenerate and rejuvenate.

I scamper back along the trail, my heart singing for joy.

Atlin Lake

When I return to the two-bedroom cabin we have rented beside the lake, I find Gerry standing in the kitchen, eating herring out of a can with her fingers. She has already emptied one tin that lies discarded in the sink. Wide-eyed and furtive, she shovels the food into her mouth, as the ruddy oil runs through her fingers and trickles down her arms. Turning her back to me, she finishes the tin and wipes her hands on a paper towel.

"Bloody hell, I was hungry," she says half apologetically, still with her back to me.

She has been gone since early morning on her fishing expedition.

"Did you catch any fish?" I ask.

"Yeah, some sorta fish called Dolly Varden."

"Good God." I can't help laughing. "That's not a fish, that's a character in a Charles Dickens novel."

She turns to face me, looking dispirited.

"Doesn't matter. I gave them to Hank and his son to take. He's leaving tonight to get home by the end of the Labour Day weekend." Her voice sounds regretful. "Whatcha been up to?"

I consider telling her the results of my expedition to the museum, but think better of it. I hand over a notice for a Labour Day barbecue being held in town tonight. "What do you think? Sounds like a lot of fun. A Robert Service poetry reading thrown in."

"Naaa," she says. "I've eaten."

Caribou and moose, the flyer promises.

"You could just have the salad," I wheedle. "Do come, Gerry, it will be a true Canadian experience."

"Can't have you missing out on a good feed, Cassandra."

I am so furious my cheeks burn. It is Gerry who eats all the time, not me. I am always catching her gorging on some strange processed food she has bought at the supermarket. And she thinks I don't know about all those laxatives she takes. Yet if I mention food she implies that I can think of nothing else.

I stride back out into the suddenly bitter wind, with an angry monologue forming in my head.

Before I started on this trip, it never occurred to me to think of myself as fat. I am as fit as Gerry, even if I don't sprint up mountains, and I am ten years older.

I refuse to concern myself any more with my body image, though God knows I used to be obsessed about it. My entire youth was spent in periodic bouts of starvation, having nightmares about being fat, making myself miserable with self-disgust, enduring a merry-go-round of fad diets that left me tired and cranky and weakened my immune system. I swore right off that negative spiral when I turned forty.

Calming down, I rehearse the reaffirming litany I have taught myself about the value of a healthy diet: complex carbohydrates, fruit and vegetables, protein and whole-wheat grains. What is the perfect size compared with good health and energy?

Gerry's remark about Hank reminds me that after Labour Day nearly everything closes down in the North. I am determined to book ahead for somewhere to stay each night, someplace where we can put some space between us.

The pay phone is enclosed in a Plexiglas box that leaves my legs and torso exposed to an icy wind coming straight off the Juneau Glacier. I have found one likely place in the *Yukon Guide*, but the phone number is very odd. I dial the operator, wait for two minutes and then listen patiently to a message, first in French and then in English, telling me to choose an operator in English or French. This is what really drives me crazy about Canada. I wait another minute or so before an English-speaking operator comes on the line and I inquire about the strange number.

"That's a radio phone, ma'am."

I ask her to connect me.

"That'll be $3.50 for the connection and $2.00 for every minute."

I give the number of my twenty-dollar phone card.

"No, ma'am. You have to pay cash or have a phone number I can bill."

"Visa?"

"No, ma'am, give me a phone number to bill."

"I'm a tourist. I don't have a phone number."

"Well, ma'am, you have to deposit a minimum of $5.50 or I can't make the connection."

This pay phone takes only quarters. She is asking me to feed the phone twenty-two quarters. Just for starters. I don't have any quarters. That is why I paid $20.00 for a phone card. Determined to sort this out, I trudge to the general store and change money for as many quarters as they can spare, return to the phone to listen once again to the instructions in French and English and wait once again for the operator. Finally I get to give the number and deposit twenty-two quarters, holding another four in reserve.

"Calling xyz 123, Calling xyz 123."

This primitive technology reminds me of my childhood, when every night before the radio news I listened to the serial *Blue Hills*, which was set on a farm in outback Australia. That was in the 1950s.

"Come in, xyz." The call is repeated several times. No response. No answering service. Nothing.

When I hang up, fourteen of my quarters clang into the cash box of the phone. Eight are returned to me. Hands trembling with cold, I consult my *Yukon Guide*. Nearly all the numbers are radio phones.

Shit. Shit. Shit.

I just want to turn tail and go home to Lower Snug.

My phone card may not work for radio phones only a few hundred kilometres away, but it will connect me across the Pacific Ocean to Tasmania.

I dial my home number.

Michael has sleep in his voice when he finally answers. He listens patiently to my tearful rant about Gerry, even though he is probably standing on the cold kitchen floor in his bare feet.

"It doesn't matter, honey bunny," he says when my explosion of resentment begins to peter out. "Pay no attention to what she thinks. Remember the reason for this trip is for you to do your research on Lillian. Isn't that so?"

"I guess you're right," I sniffle. "I am being oversensitive."

To cheer me up he tells me about the wisteria along the back fence, which has just burst into spectacular spring blossom. It all seems very topsy-turvy.

After Michael has returned to his warm bed, I stare across the lake for as long as I can tolerate the cold.

The sensible thing is to lay down a few ground rules about food, I decide at last. It is obvious that Gerry's wild mood swings and her abrupt aggression are the result of not eating. Once she eats properly, she will return to being the woman who was my friend.

Re-entering the cabin, I see the moment for confrontation has passed.

Gerry is sitting at the table holding the invitation to the Labour Day barbecue and poetry reading. She is wearing a fresh pair of jeans and a brilliant pink silk shirt. Her eyes have been outlined in kohl and her lips are glossy red.

"Better get your glad rags on," she says merrily. "Time to tuck into some of that murdered wildlife."

The young actor giving the Robert Service recital is doing a pretty fair job.

> We sleep in the sleep of ages, the bleak, barbarian pines;
> The grey moss drapes us like sages, and closer we lock
>   our lines,
> And deeper we clutch through the gelid gloom
> Where never a sunbeam shines.

"Spot on," Gerry murmurs. "Those pine forests, I just can't stand them."

Gerry is speaking to a thin girl with long fair hair and a small, pinched face. The two of them have bonded at the dessert table while comparing the relative calorific value of the lemon meringue pie versus the chocolate fudge cake. Now both plates are piled high with a large serving of each.

The new friend is a young English backpacker named Lisa, who must be much more sturdy than she looks, since she has hitchhiked across Australia and most of North America. Gerry tells me that Lisa is aiming to get up to the Arctic. My brainwave is to offer her a lift with us as far as Dawson City, so she can act as a kind of buffer in the escalating tension between Gerry and me.

The food certainly is delicious, especially the marinated caribou from the barbecue, as long as you don't think too

much about the graceful animal it once was. Vast numbers
were photographed swimming across the lake earlier in the
century. They say that the caribou herds are still large in
these parts, but I haven't seen evidence of any. No way can
I bring myself to try the moose, since I am convinced this
great, ungainly creature is now endangered by hunting.

The man who is handling the barbecue assures me that
moose and caribou are not scarce at all, just skilled at keeping
out of sight. When I point to the absence of roadkill as an
indication of scarcity, he hoots with laughter.

"You wouldn't want to hit a moose, lady. You'd be the
roadkill."

"There is plenty of roadkill," explains a pleasant-faced
young man who has joined me at the barbecue. "Highly
sought after. First pickup that comes by is out with the ther-
mometer; if the animal is still warm, it's into the back and
home for supper."

The young man's name is Marc, and he is a TV presenter
from the Canadian Broadcasting Corporation who is shooting some local colour for a Labour Day special. Marc is keen
to come to Australia, and he pulls up a couple of chairs so we
can sit down and talk about it. Balancing plates on our laps,
we compare impressions about our respective countries. When
I pour scorn on the radio phones, he explains that everyone
has radio phones because they are so far north they are out of
range of the satellites. Microwave towers provide telecom-
munications in some places, he assures me.

Gerry stands some distance away, watching this exchange.
She appears to be glaring at me. Marc also notices her
interest.

"Your friend over there told me that you are looking for
the woman who walked to Russia. You know, CBC once con-

sidered making a documentary about her, but it never got anywhere. Maybe you should check out the archives in White-horse. They have great stuff about the old days in there." Flipping open his wallet, he draws out his card, which he hands to me in case I need any help with additional research. An impatient horn blast from his cameraman sends him jogging toward the waiting CBC van. "Let me know what you find," he shouts over his shoulder.

Klondike

Some enterprising soul has set up a produce stall with an honesty box at the crossroad between Atlin and Whitehorse. Romaine lettuce, luscious red tomatoes and exploding green peppers are carelessly displayed.

"Aren't these marvellous," I enthuse, clambering down from the Pathfinder. "How much should we get?"

Gerry sits at the wheel, barely bothering to look at the produce. "You just buy whatever *you* want, Cassandra."

A few dollars drop into the box and I climb back into the passenger seat, placing a bag of tomatoes and peppers at my feet as we continue the remaining few kilometres into White-horse. Gerry and Lisa are looking forward to a few hours in Whitehorse (population, twenty-four thousand), which has a city's amenities, and have suggested they will wash the car, do the laundry and go to the supermarket. Gerry has been deprived of the joys of a supermarket for too long.

They drop me at the archives and we agree to meet again in four hours.

I don't need so much time, as it turns out. The Yukon Archives yield little more information about Lillian than I already have. The very helpful archivist takes my address in case any more material should be found.

Lillian stayed only a brief time in Whitehorse before proceeding farther north, although she did attract the attention of a journalist from the *Whitehorse Star*, who made it his business to find out about her. The first thing I notice in his account is that there is no suggestion that Lillian had come from New York. In fact the *Whitehorse Star* suggests that she may have come from Renfrew, Ontario, known to be home to a community of Polish immigrants, though that, too, is pure guesswork. The newspaper does report that she arrived in Hazelton via the steamer from Vancouver to Prince Rupert.

So she didn't walk all that way to Hazelton.

As for where she was headed, the *Whitehorse Star* ruefully conceded that Lillian was "not given much to speaking," and people she had met on her trek had been unable to ascertain where she was going. The paper had been in touch with the telegraph relay men and others who had contact with the woman, but all they could establish was that Lillian was going "a little way north of Whitehorse." No mention from anyone of Russia or Siberia. Nor is there any mention of a hand-drawn map showing a route to the Bering Sea.

I am amused to see that the paper had added, as if this were of real significance, "to the few people she met on her way north, she gave the impression of being a man-hater."

Is "man-hater" code for lesbian? I wonder.

On the scent of a good story, the *Whitehorse Star* continued to follow her progress to Dawson. "As the mystery woman passed through Carmacks, she maintained her silence," the newspaper reported. Likewise, when H. O. Lokken took her over the Peel River on the ferry, he could report that she said nothing. Further snippets of information from people who saw her yielded no intelligence about her purpose or about her origin.

It is not much to go on.

The really impressive material in the archives comes from the Klondike gold rush, stories of folly and endurance in that brief period of madness that are remarkable by any measure. The photographs tell it all.

The main route to the Klondike strike was not in fact the Telegraph Trail; it was via Lynn Canal in southeast Alaska, where the eager stampeders alighted at the tidal flats at Dyea or at Skagway. No trace of Dyea remains today, but photographs show the tidal flat transformed into a wave of expectant men and voluminous stores. The only way into the Yukon was over a formidable mountain range, following the ancient trade routes of the Tlingit. The North West Mounted Police made it a rule that everyone entering the Yukon had to have one ton of provisions, enough food supplies to tide them over for a winter that would last eight months. All those men on the Dyea flats lolling against their mound of gear—city slickers by the looks of them, eager to get on their way—had little idea of the horrors that awaited them on the Chilkoot Trail, fifty kilometres of pain and anguish climbing through a pass eleven hundred metres above them.

Stampeders might use pack dogs or bullocks, or even mountain sheep, as one photo shows, to pull their stores to the camp at the base of the mountains. In the last resort, the only way over the uncompromising summit was on shank's mare, step by tortuous step, with the stores strapped on the back. The final push to the summit was a thirty-degree slope that rose two hundred metres every five kilometres. The Golden Stair, as it was known, has given us the most famous photograph of the stampede: an antlike procession of tiny figures laden like pack horses, strung out in silhouette along the steep slope of a massive, forbidding mountain. It was like climbing an icy stairway to hell, according to one anonymous stampeder.

Looking closely at one of the photographs, I can see that a man has lost his footing and is sliding down through the legs of his companions. It might take him several hours to recover his place in the line. Once at the top, he would deposit his burden to be assessed by the Mounties and retrace his steps for the next load. As many as twenty trips were required to transport a full quota of stores.

There were women too, the photographs reveal. Martha Black kept a diary in which I read her experience of the Chilkoot: "Rocks! Rocks! Rocks! Tearing boots to pieces. Hands bleeding with scratches. I can bear it no longer. In my agony I beg the men to leave me—to let me die in my tracks."

On 3 April 1898 a massive avalanche engulfed the entire base camp. There are terrible photos of survivors digging frantically in the snow with nothing but their walking staffs; of corpses frozen in the attitude of their last moments, arms thrown up to protect their faces from the onslaught of snow. I tremble to look at them.

The White Pass from Skagway was even worse.

While not as high as the Chilkoot, the White Pass was much more rugged. Here men were tempted to take pack horses, which gave the trail its special name, Dead Horse Gulch. Some five thousand animals perished from exhaustion or broken fetlocks or being impaled on stumps. In parts the trail was nothing but rotting and broken carcasses, providing a footing for the half-starved and exhausted beasts that came after them, stumbling through a black multitude of cawing and squabbling ravens. My God, the smell! To envisage how it must have been defeats my imagination. The photographs are utterly grotesque and stomach-turning.

White Pass was gruesome but short-lived. By 1899 the White Pass Railway to Whitehorse was completed and the old Tlingit trails became part of folklore, just as the Tlingit found themselves squeezed out of their lucrative inland trade.

Getting through the mountain passes in one piece was only the first of the Klondike endurance tests; the next was to navigate the swift-flowing Yukon River to Dawson City, where the rush was concentrated. A photograph taken during the winter of 1898 shows another massive tent city on the shores of Lake Bennett, south of Whitehorse. Beside each tent is a boat of sorts, in various stages of construction. The surrounding hills have been stripped completely bare to get timber for the planking.

When the ice broke up in June 1898, an extraordinary armada of some seven thousand rickety craft set out to sail to Dawson City. In a photo taken from one of the boats, the broad Yukon River could easily be mistaken for Hong Kong Harbour with its jostle of jam-packed junks. Plenty of stampeders failed to make the distance, foundering in the rapids at various points along the route. At least 150 men drowned in the treacherous Miles Canyon, just outside Whitehorse, yet many thousands did get all the way to Dawson City.

A staggering feat, when all is said and done.

With sinking heart, I watch as the Pathfinder, washed clean of its crust of dust and mud, pulls into the archive car park. Gerry and Lisa are in high spirits, chattering away in some inane patois of their own devising. Lisa vacates the front seat for me, leaving milkshake containers and chocolate wrappers on the floor.

My presence settles on them like a lead weight.

As we head toward Dawson in the late afternoon, the landscape glows; the Yukon is an undulating carpet of gold running up into the crevasses of the grey basalt hills. The original spruce forest has been almost completely cleared, either by gold stampeders or by fire, and recolonized by balsam poplar, or black cottonwood, as it is commonly known, a particularly aggressive colonizer because it reproduces from a mat of fast-growing roots. No other trees have much of a chance. A close relative of the trembling aspen, the balsam poplar turns a rich cadmium yellow in the fall.

"You know the reason why we've seen no pine forest around here?" I start to tell Gerry and Lisa about the great boat-building enterprise of the gold rush in the photo at Whitehorse.

Adopting my didactic stance is exactly the wrong tack to take.

Catching a sigh of unresponsive coolness from Gerry, Lisa rummages in the Safeway bag to cover the tension.

"Heigh-ho, it must be time to break out the Air Crisps. What'll it be, chili or BBQ?"

Gerry opts for the chili. A large box of potato chips appears on the seat between us.

As the sky is darkening into a rosy sunset, we book into a lonely hotel that has a suite with two bedrooms—one room for me and one for my two companions—as well as a kitchenette. I know that this place is the only one of its kind along the entire highway, having done my research beforehand, but I make it seem as if we have stumbled upon it at just the right time. Gerry and Lisa had been all for sleeping out in Lisa's tent, leaving the car for me. Now both are delighted by the prospect of beds and sheets and, best of all, cable television.

I fetch the food box from the back of the car.

"I am sooo full," moans Lisa.

"Me too." Gerry pushes out her non-existent stomach and puffs her cheeks in a simulation of grossness.

"No dinner," they tell me in unison.

I am angry but not surprised, as I have counted (sternly, silently) three big packets of chips, plus two Hershey bars (milk and dark) and a tube of licorice lollies. They loll in front of the TV in the main room while I settle for a Cup • A • Soup and some cheese.

Sprawling on the couch, Lisa flicks through the many channels until she hits upon a program about weight loss. One woman claims to have lost 154 pounds.

"One hundred and fifty-four pounds," she shrieks, with lingering emphasis on every word. "I don't even weigh that much."

"I probably do," Gerry says uneasily.

"Yes, but you've got big bones. She must have been as big as you and me together. Can you imagine anyone that humongous?"

They pull faces in disgust and continue flicking channels.

I walk outside. The evening star is twinkling in a purple sky that stretches unbroken above my head. I don't believe I can tolerate this for one moment longer. Just as the Big Dipper is faintly visible in the sky, Gerry comes out for a cigarette. She gets straight to the point, saving me the trouble.

"You're obviously pissed off, Cassandra. What's your problem?"

"We just aren't suited to each other any more," I say lamely. "You and Lisa get on so much better. I think we should split up."

She draws on her cigarette and says nothing.

"You and Lisa could have much more fun without me," I repeat, trying to be generous. I notice my fingernail is bleeding where I have ripped the cuticle.

Gerry stills says nothing. After a while I see the glowing arc of her cigarette flicked into the darkness.

"What about the car?" she finally responds. "The agreement was for me to drive you to Anchorage and then take the Pathfinder back to Vancouver." Her voice sounds tremulous. "I don't see why that should change." She looks down at her feet for a moment, then raises her face to mine. "We'll be okay."

Dawson City

Next morning I rise very early. Through the window I see a blue sky, but I can tell it is not going to be a pleasant day. My nerves are shot after an uneasy sleep.

Was I snoring?

Could they hear me?

During the night I was aware of Lisa—I guess it was Lisa—forcing herself to vomit in the bathroom. Bulimia is something I have read about in women's magazines at the hairdresser. In my wildest dreams, I never expected to be living with it.

Twice over.

I reorganize my bags so I can accommodate the unused pasta, the pesto, the garlic, the hunk of Parmesan, the virgin olive oil, the tomatoes and the smoked salmon. I don't know what I am going to do with all this food, but I can't stand waste.

Gerry, bleary-eyed, catches me at it.

"Here, take it all." She is vehement, pushing more food toward me. "I don't want any of it."

I add the dreary noodles and the Cup•A•Soup box, which I tear open so I can fit the sachets in my pack. Gerry misunderstands. She thinks I want to share this miserable booty.

"No. No. No. I tell you I don't want it. I don't want it." Her teeth are clenched. Yesterday's junk-food excess has filled her with extreme self-loathing. Today she hates everyone and everything.

Soon after we leave, Lisa falls asleep; it is not soon enough for me. She wakes sporadically to natter, pleased as punch to be transported in a brand-new four-wheel drive, with all expenses paid.

We come to an abrupt stop where a river runs right beside the road, and pile out of the car to watch a young bear splashing in the water. He lifts his head and looks steadily at us. Lisa is nervous; she has not been so close to a bear before.

I have been reading about bears. Some New Age types claim that you can communicate with a bear, soul to soul. Fixing bear junior in my sights, I project a beam of thought toward him to see if I can tempt him to consider this skinny English crumpet for his supper. Indifferent to my shameful intent, he lollops into a glowing thicket of cottonwood without a backward glance.

No one else has stopped to watch the bear except for us. There is hardly another vehicle on the road. Summer is completely over. Mother, father and baby bear will soon be going to their dens.

We drive on through swaths of gold, with Lisa dozing in the back. Gerry searches for an FM radio station, eventually finding a slightly static CBC station. Through the crackle, we are treated to an archival interview with Mrs. Ellen Carver, a seventy-three-year-old who climbs to the top of a thirty-metre tower and sets herself on fire before diving two metres of water covered in flames.

"Why do you do this?" the interviewer asks.

"Well, now." Mrs. Carver's voice is still strong but has a slight quaver. "It began with my father. He used to train horses to dive from a forty-foot tower into twelve feet of water. He couldn't dive or swim himself, so he got me to ride them."

"Your father was a partner of Buffalo Bill, is that right?"

"Oh yes. But then he went out on his own with the horses. Such a showman. He didn't push me into it. I was fourteen when I started the dives."

"And how many dives have you done since then, Mrs. Carver?"

"Thirty-four thousand." She has no hesitation about the figure. "And that's not counting the forty-foot dives on horseback."

This has us both in stitches. We shoot one another a look of unadulterated delight as Gerry reaches for the volume button.

"Have you ever been hurt?"

"Nothing too serious. I had third-degree burns a few times. I always cover my mouth so I don't inhale the flames."

Mrs. Carver reflects on this. "It can be tricky if the wind is blowing in the wrong direction."

Mrs. Carver has a broken wrist at the moment, but she fully expects that it will not deter her from her dive that evening.

"Any thoughts about retirement at seventy-three?"

She gives a rich, throaty laugh. "Goodness gracious, no. I just love the work."

The program concludes with a postscript to say that Mrs. Carver made her dive but the gravity pulled out the pin in her broken wrist so, reluctantly, she had to cancel her next round of performances.

Shared pleasure in this eccentric offering opens an old channel of warmth between Gerry and me. Now, as the highway slips by, she tries to remember the words from *Annie Get Your Gun*.

Is it possible that we could start over again, I wonder?

Then Lisa comes to life in the back. "Anyone for a milk-chocolate Hershey bar?"

At the Five Finger Rapids recreation site, there are a hundred or so steps leading down to a wooden observation platform that gives a panoramic view of the mighty Yukon River. Lowering storm clouds moving in from the south cast a sombre light on the swirling milky green river, which is thickened by the fine moraine particles carried in the current. Immediately below us, the turbid water is churned into a series of whirlpools and eddies that would make short work of any flimsy boat.

No wonder so many stampeders came to grief.

It is really cold. The temperature can't be much above zero.

We bound back to the car—two steps at a time—Gerry and Lisa chattering away like a pair of canaries. In a sheltered spot, I set up the stove while Gerry reads aloud snippets from the Whitehorse newspaper she found wedged between the slats of the picnic table.

"Hey, get this. A boy fell over Niagara Falls and survived. It says he was the first person to do so without wearing protective gear."

"Why would you fall over Niagara without protective gear?" Lisa wants to know.

"People do these ridiculous things," I interject, spooning the coffee into the pot. "It's like bungee jumping."

"What's wrong with bungee jumping?" Lisa is piqued.

Too late I recall how she told us about having a great time bungee jumping in New Zealand.

"I know this may seem hard for someone like you to understand, Cassandra"—Gerry's voice is icy—"but some people actually *enjoy* things like bungee jumping."

I feel as if I have been slapped.

At Pelly River, where we stop for gas at the local band store, there is a phone booth. I am struck with a desperate need to ring Michael. I need some relief from this nightmare. I don't care what the time is in Lower Snug.

A very travel-stained youth is leaning against the booth, while inside his girlfriend is shouting reassuring words to her mother about what a wonderful adventure they are having. As there is no car in evidence and only a pair of overburdened backpacks propped beside the road, I presume they are trying to hitch a ride south. Mother must be taking the call collect. No amount of fierce looks can induce the girl to surrender the phone to me.

At the next tiny settlement of Stewart Crossing, there is no phone or any sign of human activity. Everything is closed and boarded up for the winter. It was at Stewart Crossing, I recall, that Lillian was given a small boat. Though she had no knowledge of boats, she was able to float on the swift current all the way to Dawson City.

Thirty-nine days after leaving Whitehorse, she moored her boat beside the Klondike mine railway bridge, according to the *Whitehorse Star*, after the most trying and uncomfortable hours of her long trek.

How could she have survived all those weeks sleeping out night after night? September nights are mighty cold up this far north. Maybe she got assistance from the Northern Tuchone bands that live around here. Of course there were communities of men living in mining camps along the way. I know she stayed a few days at a survey camp in Stewart where, according to the *Whitehorse Star*, "the boys cared for her for three days during a storm." If she told the men in the survey camp what she was up to, it was never reported.

Imagine. A distracted woman emerging out of nowhere to confound all those men who had been living in isolation for months.

I wish this image did not make me feel so uneasy.

In the early evening Gerry, Lisa and I survey the prospect from a bluff above Dawson, just as the rays of the sinking sun

pierce through the heavy clouds to illuminate another panorama of grey and gold, broken by the shining loops of the
Yukon and Klondike Rivers. Below us, at the point where
the two rivers meet, is the ramshackle town. I begin to think
about where we might find a bed for the night, since most
places will now be boarded up for the winter.

My concern has been anticipated. Lisa is on the case.

"The backpacker guide says there is a great youth hostel
across the river from town." She reads the description from
her battered book: "a lovely rustic site with basic four-bunk
cabins. Communal facilities with wood stove and unique
hot-water bath. No electricity. No phone. Open to the end
of September."

Scanning the far side of the river, I eventually make out
our prospective accommodation, a small cluster of rough
cabins among the wilderness.

Not encouraging.

As it turns out, the hostel is in a beautiful spot, but the
cabins, which smell of raw pine, are unheated and chinks of
light show through the shrinking planking of the walls. The
owner, a pleasant German fellow, can't believe that I want to
take an extra cabin just for myself.

"What is the matter?" he asks with a laugh. "Do you not
like one another?"

I should have agreed that, yes, we do not like one another.
Instead I mutter something about my feeling unwell and
needing to sleep separately.

"Let's get down to brass tacks here," Gerry breaks in. "She
snores."

Our German host laughs once more at our fastidiousness
and takes us to see the woodpile, where we can chop logs to
heat water for the bath and to fuel the kitchen stove. Gerry

checks the keenness of the axe edge while he explains the intricacies of the bathhouse.

"You must be familiar with this kind of bath," he tells me. "I got the idea in the Northern Territory of Australia."

"She wouldn't know." Gerry drives the axe into a log, which falls into two neat halves. "This one only likes to stay in five-star hotels."

For her part, Gerry is delighted with the place.

In my chilly cabin I lay out my sleeping bag on a bunk and put a flashlight by the bed. From other empty cabins, I cadge every spare blanket available. Once satisfied that I might survive the night in this frigid place, I pull on my thermal jacket and thick socks and walk up to the pit toilets behind the bathhouse. Passing the open kitchen, I hear two travellers screaming at each other.

"I tell you I don't want to eat." A woman's voice, nearly hysterical. "It's you, you're the one who wants to eat. I have had enough."

He yells something back at her that I cannot catch.

They are still at it when I return.

She is crying now.

I recognize them as the young backpackers I saw at the band store at Pelly River trying to hitch south. Here they are now, above the sixty-fourth parallel, with winter imminent and barely a car on the road. Not having a wonderful adventure.

How is it that people get persuaded that this kind of travelling is fun?

PART THREE

Adrift
in Beringia

Arctic Circle

It is below freezing when I awake. Too bloody cold for me to be chopping wood to heat the water. Luckily I'd taken a reconnoitre in the town last night and discovered nice hot showers in the visitors' centre, as well as a great breakfast deal of sourdough pancakes, bacon and coffee to be had at Klondike Kate's. Springing from under my many layers, having managed to dress myself under the covers, I pull on extra socks and gloves and, with a beret pulled down to cover my ears, sprint off to catch the ferry.

The mercury has crept up a few points by the time I return to find Gerry at work at the woodpile. Clean sections of wood spring apart at each well-aimed blow. She beams at me with the pleasure that comes from exertion.

"I just love places like this, where you make your own comfort," she says, between swings of the axe.

I can see that she does. A bit of strenuous labour and she can be as pleasant as pie, as if no venomous words had ever been spoken.

Lisa has gone into town, Gerry explains, in order to negotiate a lift to Inuvik, which is about eight hundred kilometres north on the Arctic Sea. She has been offered a job if she can get herself up there.

"It's such a great day. Let's drive up to the Arctic Circle. Just the two of us. We have to get to the Arctic Circle, Cassandra, you know we do."

Again the possibility of rapprochement hovers between us.

"Could you drive all that way and back in a day?" I ask cautiously.

"Easy peasy. It's only three hundred k."

Last night I vowed never to put a foot inside that Pathfinder again. In a near hysterical phone conversation with Michael, I promised him that I would give Gerry the car on the understanding that she would return to Vancouver by the time the paid rental was up, while I would fly to Alaska. Now that I'm face to face with Gerry's endearing grin, nothing looks straightforward anymore.

"Okay," I agree, giving way to my desire to rescue this friendship. "Let's do it!"

The Dempster Highway is a gravel-and-clay road, coated with calcium chloride and built above the land because of the permafrost. It is kept open all year, remarkably, with ice bridges in place of car punts in the winter. It runs through magnificent country all the way to the Arctic. Beyond the valley of golden cottonwood and olivaceous clumps of spruce are the slate grey peaks of the Ogilvie Mountains, still free of snow, with the lower slopes draped in the deep burgundy of the dwarf birch. Crimson ribbons of wild roses run up the gullies. As we pass beyond the treeline, the intense yellow of the cottonwood gives way to the softer shades of burgundy and scarlet, rust and salmon of the tundra.

We are travelling along the extreme eastern edge of Beringia, a vast area of non-glaciated tundra that stretches from Siberia across most of Alaska and terminates at the Mackenzie Mountains to our immediate northeast. During the last ice age, this area was ice-free and lay in a rain shadow caused by the massive icefields that surrounded it on all sides. A huge amount of windblown dust enabled a nutrient-rich layer of earth to establish grasslands of rye and sage stretching two thousand kilometres and linking Asia and North America by means of the Bering land bridge.

Across this vast steppe, animals travelled in both directions, gigantic creatures such as the woolly mammoth and the American mastodon. I am familiar with these prehistoric grazing animals from cave paintings in Southern Europe and drawings of excavations in Siberia. They look like large elephants with massive trunks and shag-carpet coats. What was not familiar was the giant beaver, a skeleton of which has been excavated at Old Crow, about two hundred kilometres northwest of here. From the bones, it is estimated that these creatures must have been about the size of a black bear. Having seen the devastation that the little contemporary beavers can wreak by whittling their teeth on tree trunks, I can't imagine how a giant variant could have thrived in a treeless steppe.

"Did you know . . ." I begin, then hesitate, but Gerry turns her head toward me expectantly, so I plunge on, "there used to be a giant beaver that lived up here?"

"Yeah. Saw a model of one in the Beringia Interpretation Centre at Whitehorse."

"You did?" We have kept so much to ourselves in these last few days. "Whatever did it look like?"

"It looked just like a bloody big beaver. With huge buck teeth. I tell ya, a few giant beavers would give the Canadian logging companies a run for their money." Momentarily her face loses the preoccupied frown she has worn all morning and she favours me with her dazzling grin. "I bet you didn't know they had a prehistoric camel up here too."

She is right. I didn't know.

"And a whopping monster called the short-faced bear that used to hunt mammoths about forty thousand years ago. Twice the size of the grizzly, with huge teeth and a jaw like a vise." She shakes her head in a slow, deliberate movement. "Just as well there are no more of them left."

I wait for more information, but the road has absorbed her attention once again.

We have the highway entirely to ourselves. No traffic in either direction. I realize with sinking heart that Lisa won't manage to get a lift up this road all the way to Inuvik. She'll have to come with us to Alaska.

I'll never get rid of her now.

On the far side of the mountains, Gerry pulls off where a sign indicates a marked trail. Taking a water bottle and a handful of nuts, she quickly disappears into a wine-red thicket of dwarf birch. Following, I soon discover that the trail peters out among the rust-tinted peat moss along the river, and with each step my boots subside into the layers of sodden muskeg. I grow concerned about the damage I am doing to this wild place, yet when I look behind me the muskeg has sprung back into shape, obliterating my presence. I cannot establish where the trail resumes and, since boot tracks disappear, there is no way of knowing if Gerry has been through here. Some animal tracks do show, however. I think I recognize moose tracks. Maybe caribou. Minutes later, a bear paw is clearly visible. Squatting down to determine the size of the animal, I remind myself of one salient point: I am walking alone without a marked trail in a country full of large carnivorous animals who grow well-sharpened kitchen knives on their powerful paws. The giant short-faced bear may have disappeared for good, but the Yukon wildlife survey assures me that his distant cousin is still plentiful in these parts.

My heart is thumping with real fear. I can't help myself.

It is a poor effort to turn back when I have been walking for only forty minutes, but it is with huge relief that I find the original trail and flee back to the car.

Above, the clouds are closing in and snow is falling on the high peaks.

Coffee is percolating on the stove when Gerry returns. Slinging her camera into the car, she accepts a large mug.

"I took two rolls of film since I'll never see this fantastic place again." She gives a deep sigh. "Unless I can persuade some Yukon backwoodsman to marry me and keep me for the rest of my life."

Her wistful tone tells me that she has made no joke. Solemnly she fishes in her jacket for her tobacco pouch and carefully rolls herself three cigarettes. One for now. Two for later.

I draw attention to the heavy clouds massing around the mountains.

"Yeah," she says, drawing on her cigarette and hardly bothering to look up. "Better make tracks."

The empty road throws a snaking shadow across a brilliant mixed palette of red and pinks with rare splashes of pale green from the lichen, while in the distance the mountain chain that marks the eastern boundary of Beringia is almost completely obscured by dense cirrostratus cloud. We pass a handful of graceful caribou grazing on dwarf willows, probably part of the enormous Porcupine River herd, said to be 165,000 strong and supposed to migrate through here in a vast procession anytime now. I read an account of an awesome caribou migration written in 1929, the same year that Lillian was making her trek in the opposite direction.

While trapping on tundra known as the Barrens, a fur trader named Thierry Mallet saw a streak on the horizon moving toward him, exactly like a huge caterpillar creeping over the ground. For hours he watched as the phenomenon grew to such a size that it covered many square kilometres, until it seemed that the tundra was completely hidden by the moving bodies of hundreds of thousands of caribou. The noise of their hoofs and the breathing of their lungs sounded like faraway thunder, he said. When the leading animals reached the edge of the river, just across from his camp, they paused for what seemed like an interminable moment before walking slowly down to the bank and plunging into the icy current. With a roar of clattering hooves, rolling stones and churning waters, all the caribou followed, pouring down the bank and swimming madly to the nearest point on the opposite shore. Nothing could stop the animals as they raced up the bank, the mob parting on either side of Mallet's camp. For what seemed an eternity, the astonished fur trader was surrounded by a sea of caribou galloping blindly southward. When the final young animal had passed by, its mouth open and its tongue hanging out, silence returned and the tundra resumed its desolate aspect, with nothing to show for the great herd of caribou save millions of grey hairs floating down the river to the sea.

Now that would be something to experience!

After a century of ruthless exploitation, the caribou are not so prevalent as they once were, but they continue to graze the tundra in place of the lumbering animals of the Pleistocene, which were unable to adjust when a climate change transformed Beringia. One weird-looking survivor was the muskox, an ungainly, squat animal like a small water buffalo, with a long outer coat that reaches almost to the ground and a helmet-like arrangement of horns. Despite its horns and shaggy coat, the muskox is no relation to the bison. It originated on the high plains of Northern China about two million years ago, and its descendants migrated to North America maybe 125,000 years ago.

The long hair, shoulder humps and sloping backs make muskoxen look rather grotesque, maybe even sinister, but in fact they are very vulnerable creatures. Muskoxen robes were hugely prized by fur traders at the end of the nineteenth century because of the extraordinary insulating quality of the fine, long hair beneath the coarse outer coat. They were terribly easy to hunt because they wouldn't run, but instead formed into a circle and stood passively while hunters shot them from safe range. One hunter described it as cruel butchery, without any of the challenge or exhilaration of going after moose. He advised hunters that they might save the expense of a trip to the Arctic and go hunting in their neighbour's sheep pasture.

By the 1930s the muskox was completely obliterated from Beringia.

It is not entirely fanciful that I am on the lookout for one of these curious creatures. There is a herd on the north slope of the Yukon, near Old Crow, which has been bred from muskoxen reintroduced from Greenland; like the caribou, they range as far south as the Dempster Highway. It would be a long shot to see one. My eyes sweep the gorgeous kaleidoscope of the tundra in vain.

The flooding of the land bridge did not stop all migrations across Beringia. At the end of the Pleistocene, around eight thousand years ago, lemmings invaded from Siberia, pushing across stretches of water and extensive rubble fields of sea ice. They are out there on the tundra right now, along with the Arctic foxes that hunt them, though I have yet to see one. In the winter they live below the tundra in a series of extensive tunnels insulated by the blanket of snow. Every three or four years, for mysterious reasons, the lemmings emerge from their subterranean winter homes in extraordinary numbers and strike out blindly across the tundra toward the sea. Thousands will reach a canyon or a swift-moving river, and those pushing at the rear will force the vanguard forward to their death. The seaward direction of this impetuous migration is utter madness, but shows the stamina and determination that would drive lemmings to be so widely dispersed.

The hunters who followed the huge grazing animals adapted well to the new environment, even though their prey disappeared. Across this vast steppe, people first entered the Americas, and as the ice receded many ventured farther and farther south, until their descendants had peopled both continents. I doubt that Lillian was aware of it, but she was actually making the reverse journey to that made by those very first immigrants who crossed the land bridge from Siberia more than fifteen thousand years ago.

At last a battered stone cairn informs us we have reached

the Arctic Circle, and we tumble out of the car into a freezing wind to stand on the invisible line.

It somehow seems fitting that this is also the end of the line for Gerry and me. Our friendship has reached the inevitable finale. When we get back to Dawson, I'll give her the car. She and Lisa can go off without me.

Adrift in Beringia

My first solitary day in Dawson City is crisp, clear and cold.

I move my belongings from the Spartan backpackers' hostel across the river into a pink clapboard B&B on Seventh Avenue, then load my backpack with provisions to hike up the high bluff to the northeast of the town. My new host tells me that this is called the Dome, and from there I will be able to see the top of the world.

A trail heads steadily upward through a thicket of emaciated silver trunks, where the ground is a patchwork of golden leaves, russet wild strawberries and fresh white snow glistening at its edges. A small gust of bitterly cold wind starts a shower of gold twirling gracefully through the air, brushing against my face and clinging to the long strands of mohair in my sweater. Through the thinning canopy, the sky is the colour of lapis lazuli. Occasionally I am startled by speckled ptarmigan that flap away from my boots with noisy indignation.

From the top of the Dome, I do get a marvellous view of the milky Yukon River slicing through a seemingly endless terrain of burnished gold, pockmarked occasionally with patches of dark olive spruce. Below me, great grey heaps of tailings provide sharp contrast to the intense cadmium of the regrowth cottonwood. Once again, no attempt has been made to reclaim these worked-over creek beds. Environmental considerations have never been part of Dawson's heritage.

In its heyday, during the rush of 1898–99, the city was little more than a pestilential bog of raw sewage, mud and garbage. In the Whitehorse museum I saw photographs of pedestrians wading knee-high in the muck of the streets, and wagons bogged to their axles. Typhoid was rampant. Stampeders died like summer flies. In the spring of 1899, when the ice was due to break up, concerned government officials ordered the town's garbage to be piled out on the frozen river. As the ice broke up, the Yukon swallowed what it could of Dawson's detritus and delivered the rest downstream. A novel idea to hasten the onset of the breakup was to pour sump oil on the frozen water.

The original boreal forest around Dawson was completely stripped for many kilometres in every direction, for building material and for firewood to thaw the permafrost so the miners could dig. Or else it was burnt to provide warmth through the excruciatingly long and bitter winter. In the summer of 1898, thirty-five paddlewheelers came down the Yukon from the Bering Sea, and just as many came up from Whitehorse. They could burn up whole forests just to keep the engines going. With that kind of environmental devastation, the creation of small mountains of tailings along every creek was of no consequence, simply the by-product of very basic technology.

Gold is much heavier than dirt and nineteen times heavier than water, so it easily falls to the bottom of gold pans or sluice boxes. In order to get at the gold-bearing gravel, the miner would set a bonfire to thaw the permafrost, then shovel out the earth and sluice it in a pan or rocking cradle, dumping the residue along the bank. Just as happened in Atlin, monster dredges as high as an eight-storey building were developed to chew up the creek beds and spit the tailings into steadily accumulating heaps of slag.

In the desperate search for pay dirt, many stampeders left off swishing gold in a pan to go below ground. Like lemmings, they created a series of claustrophobic tunnels that crisscrossed the tundra. Tunnelling was a particularly difficult task because the permafrost had to be thawed out by underground fires. Late at night, the main gold diggings on Bonanza and Eldorado Creeks would light up the sky with shooting sparks and flames from the innumerable mining shafts. Once the layer of permafrost had been broached, miners used pickaxe, shovel and even their bare hands to excavate damp, narrow passageways. Working by the light of flickering candles, they would painfully winch out the singed earth by the bucket load.

I imagine those tunnels are still out there, deep beneath the permafrost, another environmental nightmare waiting to happen.

Farther into the distance I perceive the landscape of Beringia as a terrestrial ocean, with rippling waves of green and gold, light and shadow, stretching to the far horizon where a saw-edge of indigo is visible. The thin, serpentine scar of the Top of the World Highway is the only sign of human impact. Somewhere along that narrow dirt road is the Pathfinder with Gerry and Lisa.

They left early this morning for Fairbanks, eager to be on their way because the road will be closed for the winter in a matter of days.

I was just as eager for them to go.

Once the Pathfinder had disappeared from sight, my relief was overwhelming. So desperate was I to escape from

Gerry's volatility and inexplicable belligerence that it mitigated any sense of loss I might have felt. Hours later, as I contemplate the road not taken, I ask myself why everything had gone so very wrong?

Perhaps it was doomed from the outset. The trip was always going to be determined by my priorities and shaped by my intellectual concerns, by my compulsive need to share my research. I was quite the wrong kind of person to be travelling with a woman desperate to be on the underside of forty. For Gerry to find herself with a travel companion who was over fifty, unconcerned about her body image and unable to resist turning everything into an object lesson, must have been more than she could bear.

Too bad for Gerry.

I actually *like* being over fifty.

I remember the day I turned fifty with enormous pleasure. It was in another stupendous landscape, in southern Austria. On my birthday a delightful Austrian academic named Adi took me hiking in the Alps. We walked beyond the clouds and crossed over into Slovenia. Above the swirling mist, where various mountain peaks represented vastly different political systems, I felt like Maria von Trapp at the end of *The Sound of Music*. Adi took a photo of me at the border marker, beaming with exertion and sheer happiness.

On the way down we stopped at a tearoom in the alpine meadow, and Adi produced a chilled bottle of champagne he'd left cooling in the mountain spring. Just as we chinked glasses, the rotor blades of a helicopter shattered the silence. It landed just beside us and two armed border guards climbed out. I nearly choked with momentary terror, aware I had entered Slovenia without a visa. But they weren't after me for violating Slovenian mountain space; they were on the lookout for gypsies crossing into Austria. They gave us a genial nod and bought themselves a beer to drink in the soft sunshine among the meadow flowers.

I'll always treasure that lovely day.

Looking about the Dome, I spy an excellent place for my picnic. Tucked behind a rock fall, nicely sheltered from the biting wind, is an old tree stump that will do me for a table. Levelling a piece of ground with my gloved hands, I set up the Tranjia stove and fill the coffee pot with the last of the excellent Colombian coffee I bought at the Granville Island Market a lifetime ago. Waiting for the coffee to percolate, I cover the tree stump with a bright Balinese sarong and lay out my goodies: Kavli biscuits, which I spread with cream cheese, and slivers of Atlin smoked chinook salmon. For dessert I arrange a pile of Turkish figs, candied mango and dried peaches, purchased from the health food shop in Stewart.

At last, a proper picnic in the wilderness!

Not that I will be able to enjoy it for long. The weather is definitely on the turn. A dense bank of cirrostratus cloud is massing on the Alaska horizon, threatening to smother the top of the world in snow. I experience a twinge of anxiety about whether Gerry will be able to get over the road to Fairbanks. But it's not my business to worry about her now, I realize with a tremor of relief.

On the door of the Dawson museum a notice states that it is closed for the winter. This is a blow. I walk back to the information centre on Front Street.

The original clapboard buildings from the gold-rush era have been beautifully restored in the main section of town, which is basically a National Historic Site maintained by the Parks Canada service. For a reason I have yet to fathom, many of the buildings in the tourist precinct have large, rectangular false fronts made of timber and painted in gaudy colours.

The information centre is wonderfully well appointed with Internet terminals, scads of videos and printed material on the historic and natural heritage of the area. Mostly the information is about the Klondike gold rush. There are a lot of quotes from Dawson's favourite literary son, Jack London. As I am the only person making inquiries, I engage in conversation with the woman who is sitting behind a counter silently sewing flower patterns using caribou hair. This process is called "tufting," she tells me.

Her own raven hair suggests that she may be from one of the Athapaskan Nations of this area, but no, Faye explains that she is in fact Mi'kmaq from Nova Scotia. She learned how to tuft when she was the postmistress at Circle, a small settlement on the Yukon River in Alaska, just below the Arctic Circle.

Faye came into the country twenty years ago; before she moved to Circle, she spent ten years living in a cabin in the wilderness, past Forty Mile, making a living by trapping lynx and marten. She and her partner now have a fish-processing plant on the Yukon in the summer. In the winter they still keep eighteen traplines, but they come into Dawson City rather than endure the fierce cold and darkness of the subarctic winter in the isolation of a cabin with no amenities. Lots of trappers came into town for the winter, she told me, leaving their cabins open and well stocked with provisions.

This reminds me of a story I read in John McPhee's classic book about Alaska, *Coming into the Country*, about Leon Crane, a young air force pilot from Philadelphia, who was forced to parachute into what is now the Yukon-Charley

Rivers National Preserve on 21 December 1943. When Crane jumped, he forgot his mittens. The temperature was at least thirty degrees below zero. He landed with no food, no gun, no sleeping bag, no mittens and no idea where he was. Crane made his way down to the river, about seven hundred metres below, and stayed by its side, waiting for rescue, for nine days. Wrapped in his parachute, he made a fire using his matches and a letter from his father, and did not sleep for more than two hours at a time in his vigilance to keep the fire burning. When he did fall asleep, he dreamed of milkshakes, dripping steaks, mashed potato and lamb chops with fat running down his hands. When he was awake, he burrowed in the snow to find lichen to chew on.

Leaving his post on day nine, Crane walked downriver until he came upon a small cabin, which was open, with split firewood and matches at the ready, as well as sacks of dried raisins, sugar, rice, flour, dried beans, powdered eggs, cocoa, powdered milk and meat jerky. It was sufficient to keep him alive through the long winter, during which he slept eighteen hours a day, like a hibernating animal in its den. In early spring the food ran out. Crane set off with a makeshift sled through brutal blizzards until he came upon another cabin with another modest cache of food. Eventually he reached a third cabin, this one occupied by a trapper, who took Crane by dogsled to the settlement of Woodchopper, Alaska. The postmaster of Woodchopper, it transpired, was the owner of the first cabin that had saved Crane's life. He was pleased it had been of use, he told Crane, as he had completely abandoned it four years before.

In the late 1920s there were probably even more cabins along the Yukon River with caches of food, so Lillian could have sustained herself this way during her epic trip down the river. Of course, in the summer the cabins would have been occupied, so people would have made contact with her.

I ask Faye, who has a keen interest in local history, if she can help me with this.

She knows nothing of Lillian Alling.

"Never came to Circle, as I've heard. Nor the Forty Mile. You'd know if she had. Folk always keep an eye out for strangers up here."

Lillian could scarcely have been missed, Faye explains. "There's always been summer fish camps all along that river."

Pleased to be of assistance, Faye dials the number of a freelance writer who is Dawson's semi-official historian.

Ken Spotswood is astounded by my query for information about Lillian.

"I have been seriously researching and writing about Yukon history and native Indian culture for over ten years now," he tells me, "and I have never seen her name or read about her exploit. I'm impressed. Tell me all about her."

This is *not* what I want to hear.

Into a Far Country

Jack London's cabin is half a block from my B&B. That is to say, the cabin where Jack London holed up for the winter between October 1897 and May 1898 has been moved from its original place on the outlying Henderson Creek and reconstructed at the edge of the tourist precinct of Dawson City. In the summer there are conducted tours, but now that winter is settling upon the town these no longer operate.

How odd that Dawson has created a one-man tourist industry out of an American who spent nine months in the place and damn near killed himself in the process. It is even more remarkable that an experience so brief and awful could have provided London with such a rich cache of stories.

Luckily, the nearby library is open for a few hours and has a comprehensive collection of books by and about Jack London, so I am able to get the flavour of his experience during that terrible winter and brief spring.

The first thing that strikes me about Jack London is what a handsome man he was. The photograph on his famous book, *Call of the Wild*, shows a young man with a faint smile at the wheel of a boat, the collar of his oilskin turned up above his ears and tousled hair flopping over his brow. I guess it is his best photograph because it's been published on the cover of nearly every one of the many biographies of him. He was a heart-stopper, no doubt about it.

Faye at the information centre suggested that Jack London was the model for the hero of the film *Titanic*. I can't see it myself. The whiff of androgyny that hangs about Leonardo Di Caprio is nowhere in evidence in the photos of Jack London. An early shot of him at Dyea, ready to set out for the Klondike, shows a plucky nineteen-year-old with his right thumb hooked in his belt and curly hair escaping from under the leather cap he has pushed back on his head. He may be smaller than his buddies, but every inch is macho.

As a hard-drinking dockhand lounging about the San Francisco waterfront in the depression in 1897, Jack London had been one of the first to hear the news of a gold strike in the Klondike. With his brother-in-law, he took a boat to Juneau and then paddled through the Inside Passage and up the Lynn Canal to Dyea. Sensibly, his brother-in-law turned back, but London persisted, taking up with three new partners to tackle the mountain pass, an experience he was to recall with remorse and shame. The memory of the poor horses, rotting in heaps, never left him:

> They drowned under their loads or were smashed to pieces against the boulders; they snapped their legs on the crevices and broke their backs falling backwards with their packs; in the sloughs they sank from fright or smothered in the slime; and they were disembowelled in the bogs when the corduroy logs turned end up in the mud; men shot them, worked them to death and when they were all gone, went back to the beach and bought more. Some did not bother to shoot them, stripping their saddles off and their shoes and leaving them where they fell. Their hearts turned to stone—those that did not break—and they became beasts, the men on a dead horse trail.

As stampeders go, Jack London was one of the lucky ones. He knew all about boats and was able to build a craft capable of taking himself and his three companions down the treacherous Yukon to arrive in Dawson just as the river ice was beginning to form.

By the end of the first summer of the stampede, Dawson City had become a lawless boom town of flimsy shacks and tents sprung from muskeg, described by a U.S. marshall as "a picture of blood and glistening gold dust . . . starvation and death." Apart from a few lucky miners, the only people making money in this hellhole were the saloon owners, storekeepers and madams who grew rich off the failure of thousands of stranded and disappointed men.

Like so many who had streamed into Dawson that summer, London found that nearly every bit of the Klondike had long since been claimed and worked over. The claim he bought, on the wrong fork of Henderson Creek, yielded nothing but backache and heartache. Then winter set in with a fury, and it was no longer possible to even try digging for gold. The temperature was below sixty degrees and blizzards raged for days on end. For nine weeks the sun never rose.

In that excruciating winter, London found his literary pay dirt: extraordinary stories of survival and death; of nobility and craven ineptitude, set in a world of natural extremity almost beyond the reach of the imagination. "When a man journeys into a far country," London wrote in one of his earliest stories, published in 1899, "he must be prepared to forget many of the things he has learned, and to acquire such customs as are inherent with existence in the new land . . . [or] he will surely die."

In London's stories, the Klondike became not so much a real place as a territory of the mind, in which his characters lived or died because of the strength or weakness inherent in their psychological makeup. In the awesome world of the subarctic, a man soon found out what he was made of. Alone in the vast emptiness of winter, with "the darkness; the infinite peace of the brooding land; the ghastly silence," London came to see himself as "a sole speck of life journeying across the ghostly wastes of a dead world . . ." and he "realizes that his is a maggot's life, nothing more."

Poor bugger.

There is a name for this state of mind, other than literary genius. A doctor would probably diagnose it as SAD (Seasonal Affective Disorder), a kind of depression that affects about twenty-five per cent of people at high latitudes. Even in Inuit culture, the winter brings on a depression they call "*perler-orneq*," which means "to feel the weight of life."

London wrote some vivid descriptions of the state of nature in which a man might come "to feel the weight of life." He was no doubt proud that he managed to pull through that winter without doing an injury to himself or to anyone else. In quite a few of the stories spawned in that experience, London seems to take perverse pleasure in killing off inept men who could not adjust to the harsh conditions. Two lazy incompetents in his savage early story, "In a Far Country," wait out the winter in a makeshift cabin on the tundra. They come to fear each other more than the vicious cold that eats away their noses and their toes, reducing them to little more than beasts. In a wonderfully Gothic scene, these two meet one another unexpectedly, while gathering sticks for the fire:

> Two peering death's-heads confronted each other. Suffering had so transformed them that recognition was impossible. They sprang to their feet, shrieking with terror, and dashed away on their mangled stumps; and falling at the cabin door, they clawed and scratched like demons till they discovered their mistake.

They do each other in, of course. Just as the spring thaw begins and life returns to the tundra.

Critics have suggested that the story owes a good deal to Joseph Conrad, which may be so, but one of London's biographers has found the germ of the story in an incident during the winter of 1898. Apparently London used his partner's axe to cut ice, and the ensuing argument forced him to move out into a neighbouring cabin. This knowledge gives what is otherwise a melodramatic and grotesquely comic story a decidedly dark edge.

SAD indeed.

Lillian Alling floated into Dawson City on 9 October 1928, thirty-one years to the day after Jack London. Since she left at almost the exact same time the following spring, their experience of the seasons would have been parallel. A lot of things had changed in the intervening years, but not the weather.

The experience of a fierce winter that lasted from October to late May would have been just as profound for Lillian as it had been for young Jack. Her previous experience of winter must have been in more benign places. In Belorussia or Poland, temperatures would have been at least thirty degrees warmer and the winter sun would still rise, however much its brightness was diffused by heavy cloud.

Winter in Beringia is painful to even contemplate.

Barry Lopez, in his book *Arctic Dreams*, says that the oral literature of the Inuit is full of nightmare images of the winter months, images of grotesque death, of savage beasts, of mutilation and pain. No summer is long enough or sufficiently beguiling to take away the fear of winter, in his view.

Up here most people simply board up their houses and businesses and head south for seven or eight months. Those who do stay are lyrical in their appreciation of the winter: the expanse of white where the trees, rivers and mountain ranges stand out bright and clear in the snow. Breathtakingly beautiful; completely silent.

What they don't say is that the cold is so intense it can shatter rocks. For months the temperature stays around forty degrees below zero. At that temperature, a person can hear his breath freezing. A gob of spit will solidify in mid-air. Any bit of moisture in the air turns into crystals, creating an ice fog that can be hauntingly lovely but eerily sinister. Lopez describes such a day in Fairbanks: "in the witless grey light, huge ravens . . . hunkered down on the tops of telephone poles in the white vapour calling in that ear-splitting caw. I never felt anything so prehistoric." The cold drives you deep into your clothing, he says, and forces the mind to retreat into itself. What was so pitiless about the winter of Beringia, in London's memory, was not the iron cold but the silence, "born in the darkness of December, when the sun dipped below the southern horizon for good," yet intensifying as the sun reappeared in steely skies. He called it the White Silence, when "all movement ceases, the sky clears, the heavens are as brass; the slightest whisper seems sacrilege."

Utterly terrifying.

Since the library is open till late tonight, I trudge back there after dinner, my warm breath vaporizing in the cold air, to see what can be gleaned from back issues of the *Dawson News*. They have some papers from the late 1920s including issues for October 1928. On 4 October a brief item indicates that Lillian—dubbed the mystery woman—is expected in Dawson any day, having pushed off in a boat eighty kilometres up the Yukon River. When she does arrive two days later, the coverage is detailed. She is said to be "garbed in a pair of brown khaki overalls, a badly torn black coat, with a man's heavy rubber boot strapped to one foot" and to be "not adept at the English language." Basically the story repeats the material that had been in the *Whitehorse Star* concerning her trek from Hazelton. It is suggested that she is about thirty-two years old and may be of Polish origin. Why she started her journey and what she is doing travelling north remain a mystery. The journalist does say that she was "unaccustomed to oars" and that the voyage down the river had been "the most trying and uncomfortable hours of her long trip."

After that I can find nothing more about her until another brief item in June 1929 to say that she had left Dawson on that day. She had worked at the hostel in winter, the journalist reported, and "persons talking to her could get no information for the reason for her long hike." Her means of departure down the river was the same boat that had been lying on the riverbank under metres of snow all winter. "She gave it out," the piece concludes, "that she was going to Nome and across to Siberia."

She gave it out.

What is that phrase supposed to convey? Lillian had refused to explain her purpose or destination over eight long months in the town. Why would she have suggested she was going to Siberia? Sounds like a desperate journalist's guesswork to me.

The Man Who Ate His Shoes

There has been a snowfall in the night.

Tucking into a mighty breakfast of fresh fruit and sourdough pancakes—happily free of Gerry's sour looks—I re-examine my file of material on Lillian for clues as to her movements in Dawson City. As well as the article by Francis Dickie, I have located three other journalistic accounts of her trek, yet not one of them has even a whisper about what she did during her eight-month stay in this town.

My only clues are in the notes from my talk with Diane Smith at the Atlin museum. She told me that according to a newspaper account, Lillian had worked at the St. Paul's hostel, which apparently was part of the Good Samaritan Hospital. Yet another source identified Lillian working for Archie Foumier, who had a dairy farm about thirty kilometres up the Klondike River. Diane failed to tell me what this source was or where it might be found.

I emerge into Dawson City's slowly warming morning to find the crystalline white surfaces of the streets and front lawns already disintegrating into mottled slush. The snow will have melted away by mid-afternoon. Winter has not arrived, yet within a month an early blizzard could bring snowdrifts metres high that would pack down to the consistency of concrete, locking people into their cabins and throwing them onto their own resources. Woe betide those not well prepared to hunker down for the next six or seven months.

A brisk reconnoitre of the fifty or so blocks that make up the town fails to locate the St. Paul's hostel. I presume that it would have been part of the Anglican diocese mission, probably established for children of the Athapaskan First Nations who were brought into town from their surrounding reserves. The church of St. Paul's, with its distinctive square tower, is still in a commanding position where the Klondike and Yukon Rivers meet, but the hostel seems to have disappeared. This is not all that surprising. Dawson has a makeshift feel, as if it were somehow temporary, just waiting to be carted away and reassembled elsewhere. Rather than being anchored securely in the earth, the buildings rest on foundations above the ground. Brightly painted false fronts that mimic the gold-rush period reinforce the sense of impermanence. A Dawson City streetscape looks for all the world like a Hollywood studio backlot.

Quite a few of the buildings have been reconstituted from elsewhere, as has Jack London's cabin, which I come upon once again in my perambulation. I wander around the perimeter of the rebuilt cabin to try to get a sense of how it might be as a survival capsule.

London was fond of that cabin, describing it as more homelike than any other place he had lived in. It is basically one room, not much more than a couple of square metres, built from felled spruce logs, with two bunks, a table and a stove for which London and his companion had stored an enormous supply of fuel. A man could lose his fingers or his nose to frostbite while getting wood in the depth of winter. They had also stockpiled a massive cache of food: sides of cured bacon, bags of dried beans, flour, oats, sugar, together with essentials such as salt, baking powder and yeast cakes. London had heard all about the risks of braving the White Silence to hunt for winter game.

Accounts of men who perished outside the security of their cabins is common in London's early stories. In "To Build a Fire," a man slowly freezes to death after his failed attempt to light a fire under a snow-laden tree, and even more gruesome in some ways is the fate of a survivor in "An Odyssey of the North." This man, an Indian, pulls himself through weeks of starvation and exposure, only to return to his cabin unrecognizable:

> The face . . . sunken and emaciated, bore very little likeness to a human countenance. Frost after frost had bitten deeply, each depositing its stratum of scab upon the half-healed scar that went before. This dry, hard surface

was of a bloody-black color, serrated by grievous cracks wherein the raw red flesh peeped forth.

In London's telling, "the grim signature of famine" is apparent in the man's hideously changed face and also in his tattered clothing, which has been cut away strip by strip to provide sustenance.

When the caribou were not to be found and even the snowshoe hares and ptarmigan proved elusive, starving men turned to eating their rawhide garments. One of the most popular stories in the historical accounts of the Yukon is that of the Anglican missionary Bishop Stringer, who was lost on the tundra with a fellow missionary in October 1909. In an extreme state of hunger, the two men cut their walrus and sealskin boots into strips, which they boiled for seven hours to tenderize, then baked over coals before eating. "The bishop who ate his boots" inspired a scene in a Charlie Chaplin movie and is an emblematic story for Beringia, where famine is winter's frightful companion and where the frozen landscape is embedded with narratives of starvation.

At these high latitudes, eating disorders take on a decidedly gruesome aspect.

Fascinating though this grisly detail is, it doesn't provide much help in my quest for Lillian.

The absence of information about her is a puzzle. Having avidly followed Lillian's trek, the newspapers fell silent about her from the moment she arrived in Dawson till the time she left. Over the long winter, when the newspapers struggled to fill their pages and the ladies' curling competition assumed newsworthy status, surely Lillian's activities would have been a likely subject. Except that she refused to talk to anyone.

Given that she was homeless and indigent, it stands to reason that she was taken in by the St. Paul's mission—even though she was Jewish—and that she earned her keep there by helping out in the hostel. This may well have been a purely temporary arrangement until she found a more permanent home. Maybe that was at Archie Foumier's dairy farm, thirty kilometres out of town.

Anyone who was thirty kilometres away from Dawson was effectively cut off from the town in winter.

How can I find out about this Archie Foumier? A search of the relevant copies of the *Dawson News* tells me nothing.

In frustration I head off to Klondike Kate's, where they do a hearty soup for lunch and where they have one of the very few public phones in Dawson.

In faraway Tasmania, I hear the message machine click on and my own chirpy voice saying that if I leave a message I'll get straight back to me. I experience a momentary panic: Where is Michael? Surely his conference is over.

A few disappointed words mumbled into the machine brings him to the receiver.

"Hello, lovely one. When are you coming home to me?"

At the sound of Michael's voice, a flood of warm feeling sweeps through my body. I am so delighted he answered. There is a rugby match on TV, he tells me, and usually nothing can tear him away from the game they play in heaven.

He checks off the list of gardening tasks I left him.

"The tomato seedlings in the hothouse have been potted out and the stone-fruit trees have been sprayed. The peas are shooting up the trellis," he reports. "I really miss you," he adds forlornly. "I miss your cooking. I even miss having to clean up your mess."

I miss him too, most dreadfully.

"I still haven't found what I came up here for," I complain, "though there are lots of other amazing stories. I have been reading all about 'the bishop who ate his boots.'"

"Those Canadians pinched that story from Sir John Franklin," Michael breaks in, with mock indignation. "He was 'the man who ate his shoes.'"

"Sir John Franklin? You mean the colonial governor of Tasmania with the porky statue in the centre of Hobart? What has he got to do with it?"

"Who is the historian in this family?" Michael sounds gleeful. "Don't you know that before he went to Tasmania, Sir John Franklin ate his shoes in the Arctic. I'll bet you a bottle of champagne I'm right about this."

Having endured years of officer training at Dartmouth Naval College, Michael is a compendium of British naval lore. I don't doubt he is right. I assure him that I will go to the library and check it out.

"And one other thing." He suddenly sounds very serious. "You are not going to Siberia. The CNN news from Russia is frightful. The whole place has gone completely to the dogs and you mustn't go there by yourself. Just get on a plane and come home to your husband. Promise me?"

"Maybe."

"No maybe, Cassandra. You are not going to go."

I have a sinking feeling that he is right about this too.
I say goodbye with salty tears trickling into my mouth.

Sir John Franklin was so gluttonous when he was governor of Tasmania that he is reputed to have eaten a whole sheep for his dinner. Sent back to England in disgrace, he sought to redeem his reputation in 1845 by taking command of a naval expedition to find the Northwest Passage through the Arctic. He was nearly sixty years old. The portrait painted prior to his departure was necessarily flattering, but even so it shows him as puffy-faced and corpulent. Franklin consumed more than his fair share of the expedition's tinned rations, which were subsequently shown to be fatally spoiled by botulism and lead solder. So it should be no surprise that Franklin was the first officer to die in the most horrific disaster in naval history, in which food poisoning followed by slow starvation took the lives of all the 129 men of the expedition.

The Franklin voyage to find the Northwest Passage and the subsequent expeditions to search for him—some almost as terrible—have long exercised the popular imagination. What Michael had alerted me to was a much less commonly known Franklin disaster, in 1821, when Franklin was a mere naval lieutenant and led an expedition across the tundra from Great Slave Lake to the Beaufort Sea, also in search of the Northwest Passage.

Back in the Dawson library, I settle down for the afternoon to read Franklin's own account, *Narrative of a Journey to the Shores of the Polar Sea*, as well as several books on Arctic exploration. I had always thought that Franklin was a dolt, propped up by his clever wife, Jane, and the tragic fiasco on the tundra in 1821 only confirms that view, even though, ironically, it was this expedition that made Franklin famous.

With two young midshipmen, a surgeon and an able seaman, plus a large group of Métis voyageurs who had been hired to paddle the canoes and carry the provisions, Franklin departed Great Slave Lake in early August 1820 to portage the canoes up to the Coppermine River. He took only enough provisions to last for ten days. The British naval command had dispatched this inexperienced lieutenant into an unrelenting wilderness, expecting the party to cover nearly a thousand kilometres by foot and canoe and pick up provisions along the way, and anticipating support for the expedition to come from the Hudson's Bay Company. George Simpson, factor of Hudson's Bay Company, had a poor opinion of the enterprise and was scathing in his estimation of the expedition leader, writing in his journal:

> Lieut. Franklin, the officer who commands the party, has not the physical powers required for the labour of moderate Voyaging in this country; he must have three meals per diem, Tea is indispensable, and with the utmost exertion he cannot walk Eight miles in one day.

Franklin himself naively presumed that a band of Chipewyans he had hired could feed them all by hunting game, but ten days after the trip began, the food was all gone and the hunters had found no game. Franklin writes that the hungry voyageurs "broke into open discontent," refusing to continue unless they were fed. Franklin threatened to have them tried for the capital crime of mutiny if anyone refused to go on, to which one replied that it was immaterial to him whether he died on the tundra or on the gallows in England. The Chipewyan chief, Akaitcho, was equally discontented, pointing out to the Englishman that winter was near and that once he was above the treeline in the "Barren Lands," food would be impossible to find. If Franklin were to go on, Akaitcho warned, he was a dead man.

Reluctantly Franklin agreed to wait out the winter, and he had the voyageurs construct a number of log buildings he called Fort Enterprise. The party spent the winter at Fort Enterprise, with the voyageurs cutting and hauling wood, ice fishing and hunting. Each one of them made the exhausting round trip of 560 kilometres to get supplies, while Franklin and his fellow officers occupied themselves writing journals and reading. The two midshipmen fought with one another over the sexual favours of a beautiful Chipewyan girl they named Green Stockings.

Early in June 1821, Franklin set off again for the Beaufort Sea, more than six hundred kilometres north. He reached the shore in mid-July, by which time the Chipewyan had turned back, leaving behind the party of five Englishmen, nine Métis voyageurs and two Inuit interpreters. Lingering on the icy shores of the Beaufort Sea, Franklin looked in vain for the Northwest Passage and failed to heed Akaitcho's warning about the early onset of winter in the Barren Lands. He waited till the end of August to return, by which time the food was almost gone and the first snow had begun to fall. Winter overcame the party in early September, and the dried food was exhausted. Franklin fainted from lack of food and was revived with soup made from the last of the supplies. Without a supply of game, they were reduced to eating the edible but nauseating lichen that grew on the rocks, which gave many of them debilitating diarrhea. After two weeks of this diet, having found no game, the men boiled the leather uppers of their old shoes to eat.

While the Englishmen carried only "such a portion of their own things their strength would permit," the voyageurs each carried forty to fifty kilograms, and several carried canoes. By October these hardy men, renowned throughout the North for their strength and endurance, were suffering exposure, exhaustion, scurvy and starvation. To Franklin's fury, they threw away the heavy canoes and fishing nets they had been forced to carry. On 4 October, five of the voyageurs collapsed. Two were left to freeze to death in the snow, while one of the interpreters simply disappeared, never to be seen again. At that point, Franklin split the party into three groups—a fateful decision that hastened the death of six more voyageurs and midshipman Hood, who may have killed himself or else been shot by a voyageur goaded beyond endurance by his petulant complaints.

By the time two of the groups were reunited at Fort Enterprise on 29 October, each man was shocked by "the emaciated figures, the ghastly countenances, dilated eyeballs, and spectral voices" of the others. Barely subsisting on a revolting diet of lichen, putrid animal bones and boiled skins, the party grew steadily weaker, their emaciated bodies swelling with fluid and their joints too stiff to move. On 7 November, with the last voyageur *in extremis*, the group was saved by the arrival of a party of Chipewyans carrying fresh meat.

Franklin returned to celebrity status in England, where the newspapers sang his praises as "the man who ate his shoes." He was promoted to captain and made a fellow of the Royal Geographic Society. It would be a quarter of a century before his incompetence resulted in yet another terrible Arctic tragedy for which, astoundingly, he was even more loudly celebrated and applauded, albeit posthumously.

I must remember to ask Michael about this. When he was taught the history of the Royal Navy's conquest of the Arctic, was attention drawn to the anomaly that nearly all the Métis voyageurs, bred tough and seasoned in the rigours of Arctic conditions, perished on Franklin's trip into the Barren Lands, while the soft-bellied, unfit and inexperienced Englishmen survived, except for one suicide/murder? If that curious aspect of the story was noticed at all, I would guess it would have been attributed to the moral strength and genetic superiority of the English, rather than the more sinister explanations that suggest themselves to me.

The Content of the Kettles

The attraction of the top of the world is fast diminishing.

On my third chilly day in Dawson City, the Internet terminal at the information centre most excites my interest. The bookmarks are a multitude of Yukon and Alaskan tourist attractions; however, when I tap in the Web address of the American-Russian Centre at the University of Alaska, I pull up their on-line quarterly bulletin, *The Russian Far Eastern News*.

Michael was right: the news is frightful.

Under the heading "The ruble fall, falls, falls," the editor details how the Russian economy is in a tailspin, with a devaluation of the currency so enormous that the government responded by printing 188 million rubles in one week. To make matters worse, the editor observes, the political situation is just as unstable as the ruble.

This is very disheartening. I have heard nothing of this on the radio, where the news reports have been almost entirely preoccupied with North American domestic concerns.

As I scroll down, I read that the outlook is especially grim in Chukotka province, which is where I am headed. The Russian government simply cannot sustain remote Chukotka, the newspaper reports say, and circumstances there are truly shocking. Fuel shipments are totally inadequate, wages and pensions haven't been paid in months, and while people have been able to subsist through the summer on fishing and homegrown vegetables, basic food items are so scarce that restaurants and stores have been closed. Even more worrying are the expected "lengthy blackouts and heating outages" over the winter. Aging and poorly maintained nuclear power plants along the Chukotka coast are breaking down and releasing radioactivity. If the Siberian people are to survive the winter, the editorial concludes, humanitarian food aid from the United States is essential. An emergency appeal for food has been circulated, and the National Bank of Alaska has set up collection boxes at all of its branches.

In a nutshell, this means that if I go to Providenija the trip will be cheap as chips, but I will be very cold and have nothing to eat. Moreover, I may suffer radiation exposure or, at the very least, respiratory problems, since there are raging forest fires in the region so extreme that two million hectares have been labelled an ecological disaster area by the United Nations. An estimated thirty million tonnes of carbon dioxide have been pumped into the air.

The throwaway line one hears so often these days, that Russia is a "basket case," takes on a new, savage meaning. The very thought of people whose lungs have already been damaged having to endure seven or eight months of a fierce winter in Beringia with no food and no power gives me sympathetic chest pains.

At various times this century, communities on both sides of the Bering Sea have been decimated by influenza. Conditions look to be ripe for another pandemic.* Michael need have no worry. The decision about Siberia has been made for me. A recent update to the bulletin informs me that "due to recent circumstances with the Russian economy," Alaska Airlines has suspended all its services to the Russian Far East, including the weekly flight to Providenija.

Whew!

The Internet terminal also allows me access to Hotmail. For the first time in three weeks, I can get e-mail. There are two items of special interest, responses to requests I sent to Alaskan historical societies before I set out. The Circle District Museum confirms what I had been told by Faye, Circle's one-time postmistress, that nothing is known of Lillian in that town. From Eagle, only a short way downstream from here, just inside the United States border, the response is very warm and welcoming. They have no information to suggest that Lillian ever came to Eagle, but I am encouraged to visit their museum, said to be the best in the state.

The Eagle Historical Museum Web site leaves me in no doubt that it is indeed a beautiful place. The photo that arrests my attention is of the Norwegian polar explorer

---

*In the winter of that year, Providenija was placed under quarantine because of a virulent outbreak of influenza, while another town in Chukotka had to be evacuated when the heating system for the town exploded, leaving ten apartment buildings without heat in minus-fifty-degree weather.

Roald Amundsen, taken sometime after he appeared there with his dogsled on 5 December 1905, a day so cold that the town's tailor froze to death. His ship was locked in the ice in the Beaufort Sea, about five hundred kilometres to the north, and he had sledded down several frozen rivers to reach Eagle, where there was a U.S. communication base. In his accented voice, he had asked for the telegraph office, where he wrote out a cable to Norway announcing that he had discovered the Northwest Passage.

Amundsen sits on the edge of a sofa crowded with fussy cushions. He looks seriously into the camera while holding a bowl from which he is eating his first meal of fresh food in many months. He is a small, wiry fellow and his hair is beginning to recede. Enormous sealskin boots that cover his legs to the knee are resting on a richly patterned oriental carpet. I take this as a mark of the guest's importance, as most visitors to a home such as this would be required to remove their boots.

The hero status that Amundsen enjoys in Eagle, Alaska, interests me. The British, and by extension we Australians, have never been too keen on Amundsen. Six years after he had discovered the Northwest Passage, he beat our man Robert Scott to the South Pole.

Yet Amundsen surely was heroic.

Canny, too. Having immersed himself in every single account of the British Navy's tortuous search for the Northwest Passage, Amundsen deduced that it might be possible to get from Baffin Bay to the Beaufort Sea, and he then sailed through in his tiny sloop, *Gjoa*, without a serious misadventure. As the boots proudly displayed in the photograph indicate, Amundsen was never driven to consume his footwear.

Franklin had set out with all the technological advances the British Navy could muster, three years' supply of tinned food and invincible ships with reinforced hulls. Nothing could go wrong, he was supremely confident. His two ships, *Erebus* and *Terror*, were last seen by a whaling captain on 26 July 1845 anchored to an iceberg in Baffin Bay. It took many years and many search expeditions before any explanation could be found as to what had happened to Franklin and his men.

It was John Rae of the Hudson's Bay Company who found the first evidence, having come across several groups of Inuit who told him that a large group of white men had died of starvation near the Great Fish River four years earlier. The Inuit had relics from the expedition, such as silver forks and spoons and a small plate engraved "Sir John Franklin, KCB." They also told Rae of the terrible circumstances of the white men's desperate struggle to survive. The mutilated state of many of the corpses and the contents of the cooking kettles, Rae reported, made it apparent that the survivors had resorted to cannibalism.

His report was rejected out of hand by Franklin's indefatigable widow and by many prominent Englishmen, including Charles Dickens, who argued that the flower of the British Navy could never have been reduced to alleviating their hunger in this shocking fashion. Dickens attacked the treacherous Inuit who gave Rae the story, but fifteen years later Charles Francis Hall was to hear again the tales of cannibalism. This time the Inuit spoke of boots filled with cooked human flesh, bones cut with saws, skulls with holes in them, and skeletons carefully stripped of all flesh. Such reports were abhorrent at the time. During the last few decades, forensic science has proved that the Inuit were indeed reliable witnesses.

Scientific examination of skeletons found at the campsites of Franklin expedition survivors at Booth Point and at Erebus Bay, in the Northwest Territories, has revealed the

pitting that is symptomatic of scurvy. The evidence, however, also points to parallel knife marks consistent with but-
chering, and fracture marks showing that the skulls had been
forcibly broken open. Now, there can be little doubt that as
those poor men struggled across the ice, having abandoned
their ice-locked ships and poisoned rations, they did the only
thing they could to keep themselves alive: they ate the frozen
bodies of their dead companions.

One of the hideous ironies that has emerged as scholars
piece together the evidence is that the final party of desperate men, dragging their boats across King William Island
toward the Great Fish River, frostbitten, sick with scurvy
and gangrene, blinded by snow glare and in the final stages
of starvation, must have found the Northwest Passage. The
knowledge was of no use to them; they all died before they
reached the river. A parallel irony is that the Northwest Passage has never been of any use to anyone.

How readily one becomes morbidly obsessed with the
starvation narratives that saturate this landscape.

I pull my thoughts back to the task at hand in Dawson
City.

Three people are on duty at the information centre, and not
one of them knows anything about Archie Foumier or a dairy
that used to be up the Klondike River. Indeed, the idea of a
dairy way up here induces incredulity in one young man. It
may not be credible in the era of refrigerated transport, but
only yesterday I was reading how Jack London was desperate
for milk when he was here in 1898. Big money could be made
if you were able to supply such luxuries. A dairy was some-

thing for which there was once a pressing need, though I do agree that it hasn't been the case for many decades.

No one with the name Foumier can be found in the Yukon phone book.

A dead end, by the looks of it.

Maybe the local Han people (a small Aboriginal group living along the Yukon River) will have a longer memory about such things. Across the road, alongside the river, the Han Cultural Centre is taking shape.

This impressive modern building is being built with money from the recent Yukon Land Settlement, which included a substantial monetary compensation package to the Yukon First Nations of some \$250 million to be paid over fifteen years. It was a one-size-fits-all settlement that has given them title to twenty-six thousand square kilometres of land and surrendered native title on all non-settlement lands.

The beautiful wooden building is glaringly out of kilter with the turn-of-the-century architecture of the town, and my queries about it at the information centre bring very terse replies. Though the structure is complete and the new turf laid out around it, the centre will not be open till next summer.

There is nothing for it but to wander about town and look at the native art galleries. Athapaskan beadwork is wonderful, especially the elaborate floral designs for which the Han are famous.

I linger for a long while over a pair of beaded moccasins, which are exquisite but way beyond the capacity of my weak Aussie dollars.

"I am just going outside; and may be some time."

These were the last words of Captain Oates when he left Robert Scott's ill-fated polar expedition to die in the snow on 16 March 1912. It is a classic line, now in common use in Australia as an ironic throwaway remark.

I find myself repeating Oates's words in my head with a very different purpose.

To lie down in the snow like that is said to be a good way to go. Hypothermia is a gentle, rather than a painful, death. At least that is what I read in Jack London's stories.

Why wasn't that what men did when they were stranded in the icy wastes with no food and no prospect of rescue, instead of struggling on in unspeakable pain and horror?

Why was Oates the exception rather than the rule?

Survival instinct must be a mighty potent thing.

Such thoughts bring me back to Franklin's account of his expedition across the tundra in *Narrative of a Journey to the Shores of the Polar Sea*, and to the way in which all those Métis voyageurs died. In most cases, their bodies were irrecoverable.

What happened out on the tundra when the parties split up?

Franklin had dispatched midshipman Black and three of the strongest voyageurs to try and locate the Chipewyans, while Dr. Richardson stayed behind with midshipman Hood and seaman Hepburn. Franklin trudged ahead to Fort Enterprise with the rest of the voyageurs, but four of the voyageurs, unable to continue, turned back to join Richardson's group. That was the last Franklin ever saw of them. More than three weeks later, only Richardson and Hepburn made it to Fort Enterprise. They were in far better condition than anyone else, even though they had found no food other than one ptarmigan.

Franklin reports the horrifying story Richardson told about how one of the voyageurs, a part-Iroquois named Michel Teroahaute, had cannibalized the other three Métis voyageurs and had supplied the unwitting Englishmen with human flesh that he said was caribou, killed by a wolf, that they thought tasted strange. No one saw Teroahaute shoot midshipman Hood, who was holding the gun in his own hand when his body was found, but Richardson formed the opinion that the voyageur had killed Hood and was dangerously insane. Richardson and Hepburn ambushed Teroahaute and killed him, so Franklin reports.

Few people have questioned that account.

What seems an unavoidable conclusion to me is that Richardson and Hepburn could not have survived unless they had been prepared to consume the bodies of their companions. Even one of Franklin's most devoted biographers admits to a question mark over this incident, noting that midshipman Black was reported to have said that things had happened out on the tundra "which must not be known." Moreover, there were dark hints throughout the Hudson's Bay Company that Michel Teroahaute was not the only cannibal in the expedition. When Farley Mowat examined the story for his *Top of the World* trilogy, he, too, came to just that conclusion.

The phone rings just once in Lower Snug, Tasmania, before Michael answers. He has been waiting anxiously for my call, so I am pleased to be able to reassure him that I will not be able to go to Siberia.

"I'm so despondent," I tell him. "It's a wild-goose chase up here. Lillian's trail has gone completely cold. She didn't even get as far downriver as Eagle, let alone go to Siberia."

"Why are you so sure she was going to Siberia? It always sounded crack-brained to me. Maybe she was just going to someplace in Alaska."

Michael's scenario isn't a great deal of comfort, so I change the subject to my return to Vancouver. My husband wants me to fly straight to Vancouver from Whitehorse, while I want to get to Alaska and take the Alaska ferry down the Inside Passage. We argue the point for a bit, until I promise to check out the options as soon as I hang up.

"Speaking of checking things out," he adds, "what about Franklin as the man who ate his shoes? Was I right?"

"Mmmm. Not only did they eat their shoes, I reckon those naval officers ate their Métis porters."

I hear Michael make an odd noise in his throat and there is a pause.

"I think it is high time you came home, Cassandra."

A River of Defeat

The whole river seemed to pick itself up and start down the stream. With increasing motion the ice wall broke in a ringing and crashing of uprooted trees . . . great blocks [of ice] were spilled inland among the thrown and standing trees and the slime-coated flowers and grasses like the titanic vomit of some Northland monster. The sun was not idle, and the steaming thaw washed the mud and foulness from the bergs till they blazed like heaped diamonds in the brightness, or shimmered opalescent-blue.

The spectacular breakup of the Yukon ice in May 1898 was the signal to Jack London that the interminable winter had passed and he could quit his isolated cabin on Henderson Creek. His steady diet of beans and bacon had begun to kill him.

For all the grim stories of starvation, a terrible irony of life in high latitudes back then was that a person was more likely to die from food than from hunger. Scurvy, caused by a chronic lack of vitamin C, was far and away the biggest killer in the North. London described the disease as an insidious process of physical disintegration.

> In the absence of fresh vegetables and exercise, their blood became impoverished, and a loathsome, purplish rash crept over their bodies. . . . Next, their muscles and joints began to swell, the flesh turning black, while their mouths, gums, and lips took on the color of rich cream.

London was entering the fatal stages of scurvy when the river ice began to break up. Although he could barely stand and was in constant pain, he managed to build a raft out of the logs of an abandoned cabin nearby. Keeping a watchful eye for felled trees and the chunks of floating ice, he steered his raft down the river to Dawson and hobbled into the makeshift hospital of Father Judge, "the Saint of Dawson." Father Judge was able to provide London with a diet of vitamin-rich food plus the sage advice that he should get out of the Yukon as quickly as possible, or else he would certainly die.

Miraculously, within a week London was back on his feet. Since he had no money, the only way out of Dawson was down the Yukon River to the Bering Sea. He built himself yet another boat, which was, by his own admission, "homemade, weak-kneed and leaky" and which he named *Yukon Belle*. With two other disillusioned miners, London pushed off in the *Yukon Belle* on the afternoon of 8 June 1898.

According to Charmain London, who wrote the first biography of her late husband, Jack London came to understand that the Klondike could be a literary gold mine while he was "floating half-frozen down the river of defeat." During the three weeks it took to reach the Bering Sea, he began a diary, which was later published by his widow in the first volume of her autobiography in 1921.

London and his companions travelled by day and night, each taking turns on the watches. The river was treacherous, as there was still floating ice along its whole length, yet by the time they crossed the Arctic Circle, five days after leaving Dawson, they were sweltering under the summer sun. They were also nearly demented from attack by millions of mosquitoes. To fend off these winged vampires, they burnt smudges, smeared their bodies with clay and erected a tent of netting. Nothing seemed to work. The mosquitoes could bite through overalls and heavy underwear, and even the net proved ineffective. One night London's companion on the watch swore he saw a party of mosquitoes rush the netting in a body, with one of the gang holding up the edge while a second gang flew under and went to work.

Ten days out of Dawson, London's scurvy reappeared, to cripple him from the waist down. Thankfully, Anglican missionaries at Ankiv were able to provide a few vegetables, which helped London to straighten his legs and allowed him to stand without collapsing. "These few raw potatoes and tomatoes," he wrote in his diary, "are worth more to me at the present stage of the game than an Eldorado claim."

The final challenge of the trip was to navigate the mouth of the Yukon, where the river separated into a maze of channels and where a boat could be easily lost without ever reaching the ocean. London was a highly skilled sailor, and he successfully negotiated the right channel into the Bering Sea, arriving at the port of Saint Michael on 30 June. There he took a job as a stoker on a ship bound for San Francisco.

Sparse though it is, London's diary assures me it would be possible to sail a small boat the full length of the Yukon to the sea—that is to say, it was possible for three experienced hunters, one of whom was a sailor, travelling night and day for three weeks and resupplied by the missions and fishing camps along the way. Was it possible for a lone woman without a gun, unaccustomed to boats and in a flimsy craft that had lain under the snow all winter?

Using London's account, I cross-check each of the settlements at which London stopped against a guide to Alaskan communities. Many of those summer fishing camps had become established villages by the late 1920s, with a mission school, trading post and post office. Some even had hospitals. I cannot see how a woman could have taken a small boat the length of the Yukon in 1929 without being noticed by people who might have left a record of it: missionaries, schoolteachers or community nurses. Yet there appears to be nothing of this kind about Lillian.

She could hardly have been missed at every place.

Nor would it have been possible to get a ship from Saint Michael, Alaska, to anywhere. In 1898 Saint Michael was booming as the most northern port for the all-water route to the Klondike—by steamship from Seattle or San Francisco to Saint Michael, and then by a sternwheeler up the Yukon. More than thirty steamboat companies had formed to operate on the Yukon, but that traffic progressively declined until 1925, when the U.S. military post closed and steamboats were abandoned to rot on the shore. By 1929 the bustling port had become a small Inuit village. To get from Saint Michael to Wales, Alaska, the nearest point to Siberia, would require a further arduous six-hundred-kilometre trek around the shores of Norton Sound and across the tundra of the Seward Peninsula.

I can't see how Lillian could have done it.

It *is* crack-brained to think that Lillian was going to Siberia. The vast majority of Jews in Russia were destitute and frightened, having been subject to brutal pogroms in the czarist period. Violent campaigns of propaganda and persecution against Jewish religion and culture by the Soviets increased in intensity in the late 1920s. A vast exodus had brought close to a million Jews from Belorussia to America by the time Lillian arrived. She herself probably came to the United States from Poland, as the *Dawson News* had suggested, since Belorussia was divided between the Soviet Union and Poland from 1921 until 1939.

For Lillian to return either to Belorussia or to Poland via Siberia, she would have had to traverse more than two-thirds of the globe. On foot, she would have travelled for many years, and it would have been more expensive, and infinitely more dangerous, than to go back the way she had probably come, as a steerage passenger on a Hamburg liner.

It is true that deportations of Jews had begun in the late 1920s, and, possibly, people from shtetls in Belorussia were sent to Siberia. Maybe Lillian was trying to reach family members deported to Siberia, but it is hard to see how she would have known about that. She just may have heard about a proposal to develop a Jewish settlement in Far Eastern Siberia, with support from Jewish organizations in America, although this is also highly unlikely, since the project was launched two years after she set out. The last possibility, equally tenuous, is that Lillian was trying to get to family members trapped in Vladivostok trying to emigrate. During the First World War and the civil wars that followed, many Russian Jews chose a much more circuitous route, through China, to get out of the Soviet Union.

The more I try, the less success I have in finding a credible explanation why Lillian should seek to return to Russia.

As I said, the woman was clearly unhinged.

In the Dawson library, I reconsider all of the material I have collected to see where it was that Lillian said she was going, and I notice that there are no contemporaneous accounts in which Lillian actually stated her destination.

In the memoirs of the linemen, Lillian said nothing about what she was doing. The *Whitehorse Star* reporter, who had the most comprehensive coverage, was frustrated in his efforts to get any information, reporting that Lillian was not given much to speaking and that questions from strangers seemed to disturb her. "If she knows where she is going," he wrote, "she is not telling." He spoke with the couple who gave Lillian a lift between Carcross and Whitehorse; they said she gave her destination as "a short way north." The conclusion of the *Whitehorse Star* was that Lillian was running away: "Her general demeanour resembles that of a haunted person, who is ever trying to get farther away from the object of her fears."

In Dawson Lillian remained tight-lipped, giving out no information about herself or her purpose. The *Dawson News* found her to be "of a retiring nature . . . not adept at the English language." During her long stay in the town, "persons talking with her could get no information as to the reason for a long hike into unknown country."

The first time Siberia is mentioned is the day after Lillian left Dawson, when the *Dawson News* reported she "gave it out" that she was going to Nome and then to Siberia, although the paper is careful not to quote her. I have another article on Lillian from the *Yukon News*, written only last year, which quotes an old-timer who used to work for the *Dawson News*. He said that when Lillian left Dawson City, she was heading down to Eagle and that she was never heard of again.

The story about going to Russia via Siberia can be sourced to a highly coloured account of Lillian's trek in the journal of the British Columbia Provincial Police, *Shoulder Strap*, written in 1948 by a freelance writer named J. Wellsford Mills. Mills's reconstruction of events reads like a clumsy short story, with Lillian as a Russian girl adrift in New York "who yearned once more for the rugged steppes of her native land." According to Mills, "she could almost smell the barnyards . . . hear the excited gutturals of the peasants as they thronged around the marketplace listening to the latest edict of the Commissar." Overcome by nostalgia, the girl decided to walk home, since she did not have the money for a steamer passage.

Not one piece of evidence is provided.

Reading it over again, I can see that J. Wellsford Mills had no idea how this woman got to be at the number two cabin on the telegraph line in September 1927. How much he knew about her intentions when she was arrested by the provincial police is a moot point.

I can find no evidence that Lillian's statements were ever recorded by the provincial police or the Hazelton court, so I must assume that Mills interviewed Constable Wyman. I further assume that Wyman supplied Mills with the information he used to construct a dialogue in which Lillian tells Wyman emphatically, "I am going to Siberia." Mills must also have interviewed one of the linemen, Jim Christie, who is credited with the photos that accompany the piece. From Christie's information, Mills reconstructed Lillian's journey from cabin to cabin. "At no time was she communicative," Mills writes. "She told nothing of her past." Mills's story comes to its end at Dawson City. "Extensive inquiries have failed to discover her eventual fate," he concludes.

Mills's account was cannibalized by Francis Dickie for his article in *True West* in 1972, in which he has Lillian say to Constable Wyman, "I go to Siberia." The elements of the encounter with the provincial police are the same in the Dickie article, but the actual dialogue is somewhat different. I very much doubt that Wyman was reinterviewed by Dickie nearly fifty years after the event, and suspect that Dickie was engaged in some literary manipulation of Mills's original text. Another journalist writing about Lillian for *The Toronto Star*, in 1985, takes this imaginative licence one step further. He also quotes the provincial police, and his quotes are different again from both Mills's and Dickie's. In *The Toronto Star* account, Constable Wyman says, "I had a time getting her to say her name. She wasn't going to say anything to any-body . . . but I finally got it, and when she said she was going to Siberia I couldn't say anything. I thought she was out of her mind." It is most improbable that this journalist had tracked down and reinterviewed Constable Wyman, who would have been in his late eighties or even older.

As I see it, a great deal of imaginative reconstruction was used in all three journalistic accounts. There is not a scrap of hard evidence in any of them.

I try some imaginative reconstruction of my own.

"Lillian Olejnik, Belorussia," she might have said in a heavy Yiddish accent when questioned by the British Colum-bia Provincial Police. Belorussia (bee-low-rew-see-ah) was not a place that Constable Wyman would be likely to recog-nize. When he "finally got it," what he might have under-stood her to say was "me go Russia." Asked about this some fifteen years later, Wyman still remembered Lillian telling him that she was heading for Russia, the closest point of which is Siberia.

Now that makes sense to me.

Still, it doesn't get me any closer to understanding Lil-lian's purpose, nor what happened after she pushed off into the fast-flowing, icy Yukon River in June 1929.

London's stories give some idea of how treacherous the swift current of the Yukon could be for the unwary, especially close to breakup when it was full of sweepers—branches and trees brought down by the ice—and large icy chunks that could combine to form a fatal river jam. Just such a jam is vividly described in the *Dawson News* of 16 February 1906, as an explanation for the disappearance of a large party from Dawson who went downriver in a scow.

A woodcutter named George Finnegan described a funnel-shaped death trap of ice and debris that formed in the Yukon at a point where the river narrowed, not far beyond Dawson. He explained that the walls of the funnel forced the swift current through a progressively narrowing channel at great velocity until it became like a millrace, ending in a whirlpool twenty metres across, into which the river dashed with the noise and speed of a train. Any boat would be upended in an instant to reappear about a kilometre farther downstream, smashed to smithereens. Not even a dog could have escaped, in Finnegan's view.

According to the *Dawson News*, the Yukon ice broke up on 7 May 1929. A month later, when Lillian left, ice would still have been in the river. Departing down the Yukon River at the same time of the year, Jack London reported "evidence of the ice run all along the line," with islands swept bare of their trees and treacherous piles of ice-felled debris collecting at narrow points in the river. Spring floods were another cause of concern for him.

Unlike London, Lillian had no experience of boats, and the flimsy craft she took was probably unseaworthy.

Why ever did the Royal Canadian Mounted Police let her go?

"Pardon me, ma'am."

I look up to see a lanky young man in his mid-twenties towering over me.

"Are you Cassandra?"

I nod.

"From Australia, right? Looking for Lillian Alling?"

"How did you know that?"

"Not much escapes people in this town once the summer visitors have gone." He inclines his head in the direction of the pleasant woman at the library desk who had allowed me to borrow Jack London's stories. "The librarian told me about you." A long arm shoots down to shake my hand. "My name is David."

"Nice to meet you, David. What are you up to in Dawson?"

"I'm a graduate student of media studies from the University of Alaska, in Anchorage. I'm doing my thesis on the cultural commodification of the Klondike stampede. Been working in the archives over the summer as a volunteer." From under his left arm he pulls a slim manila folder. "I found you the file on Lillian Alling. It's not much, I know."

"Oh, David," I enthuse, "I am pitifully grateful to you."

He pulls up a chair beside me, and I eagerly flip open the folder. My enthusiasm evaporates as I find copies from newspaper cuttings that I've already seen. The one small item of interest is a letter from Clifford Thomson sent to the research librarian to say that in 1928 he was asked by the *Whitehorse Star* to report on Lillian and saw her arrive in October. He took two photographs. "I endeavoured to have a talk to her," he writes, "but she became very angry and refused to talk." He did not know what she did in Dawson over the winter, but he did witness her departure in her small boat the following June.

"So that's it, then," I sigh, closing the file and handing it back.

"As far as I can tell."

"No photographs?"

David shakes his head.

"So she just disappeared?"

"When I heard about you, I e-mailed a guy who used to work in the archives here. He says there was a woman film-maker came up here from Vancouver a few years ago looking for the same person. She drew a blank as well. Wrote to the post office of every community along the river. Nothing."

I put my head in my hands and sigh one more time.

"How are you getting back to Vancouver?" He sounds concerned.

"I don't know." As I look up, I am mortified to feel the prick of tears behind my eyes. "I had planned to fly to Anchorage to get the Alaska ferry but it has stopped running from there. I have to go to Haines or Skagway to get it." I blink the tears away. "I could fly to Fairbanks and catch a bus. Trouble is, I can't get a plane for three days."

"This must be your lucky day." He runs long fingers through the thatch of tawny hair that has flopped over his brow. "I'm leaving for Anchorage tomorrow morning. I can drop you at Tok and you can catch the bus to Haines from there."

"You mean it?"

"Sure I mean it. I'd appreciate someone to share the cost and I can pick your brains about Australia. I really want to go to Australia."

David unfolds into a beanpole and replaces the folder in his armpit. "You're staying at the White Ram B&B, right? I'll come for you at 8 a.m."

The Top of the World

The top of the world is bathed in sunlight. In one more day the road will be closed, yet there is no sign of snow on this dazzling morning. Cruising along in David's Toyota, I feel as if I am adrift on a gently undulating sea, with the morning sun creating waves of light and shadow, a chiaroscuro of ochre and indigo, flowing in every direction.

We stop at the Alaskan border to present my passport to a cheery immigration official. I have been coming and going through America for the last thirty-five years, and this is the first time I have met an immigration official who isn't hard-faced and rude.

"That will be $10, thanks, ma'am," he says, smiling broadly. He stamps my passport with the image of a caribou and waves me through. "You have a good day. Enjoy our great country."

I happily assure him that I will.

On the American side of the border, I notice a new phenomenon. The country is crawling with hunters. The first one is just over the border, curled up in the cabin of his truck in a sleeping bag, his gun at the ready. Past the trading post at Chicken, men with guns can be seen at every pull-off on the highway. These hunters are exceptionally good-humoured, just waiting and watching. In the back of their pickups, they have four-wheeled motorbikes called ATVs for burning across the tundra to reach their target.

"I thought the moose season was finished," I say, doing my best to sound knowledgeable.

"You never can tell in Alaska." David reaches across to the glovebox and extracts a book of Alaskan hunting regulations. "It changes from place to place."

The Alaska Hunting Regulations Number 39 is 112 pages long. The cover has a wonderfully folksy photograph of a hunter walking away from the camera through the snow, with his gun over his shoulder, followed by two tiny children, each carrying a snowshoe hare, which dangle the full length of their small bodies.

"The family that hunts together stays together," I remark archly.

"It's a way of life up here," David replies with easy grace. "As natural as breathing."

Once I identify which game management area we are in, I am able to establish that the season is still open for caribou— one bull per hunter—and for wolves—five per hunter. There is open season on black bears, while it is possible to shoot a grizzly bear once every four years. As for the elusive moose, a male with an antler spread of fifty inches and at least four brow tines—the points on the front of the antlers—can be taken for a few days yet.

Before the hunter can legally shoot his one bull moose, he must first accurately identify the size of the antlers and count the number of brow tines. If you're not sure, the booklet sternly warns the hunter, do not shoot. Having established that he has shot the right male animal of the right age, the hunter must salvage and remove all of the meat. A wanton waste of game meat is an extremely serious offence, punishable by a fine of up to $5,000 and one year in jail. Moreover, he must leave the penis, scrotum and testicles naturally attached to a part of the rear quarter to show the sex of the animal. Antlers alone are not proof of sex. A live adult moose can weigh up to 1,650 pounds, so salvaging the meat is a massive job.

I am impressed with these rigorous restrictions, though I wonder who is out here to enforce them.

"A lot of hard work to get moose," I observe.

"Like I say, a way of life. It is inconceivable that you would go through the winter without having first bagged a moose to tide you over."

David tells me that he doesn't care for hunting, but his roommate is a keen hunter and they will have plenty of game meat to get them through the long, cold months.

"My roommate likes to hunt bears."

I wince.

"He hunts the traditional way," David continues, oblivious to my discomfort. "With a bow and arrow."

"You mean those mechanical crossbows."

"No way. They don't allow a crossbow or any electronic bow. Nor can you use a scope or any devices to enhance the optical magnification. Basically you're only allowed to hunt bears the way the Indians did. If you are up for that, you can have one fully grown male grizzly every four years and one black bear each year. As long as it still has its penis attached."

I purse my lips in disapproval and continue to flip through the book, discovering that my favourite animal, the lynx, can be shot throughout Alaska during the winter. Lynx are survivors from Beringia; they resemble large, wily cats, except that their ears have long tips of hair like waxed moustaches. The most wary of all woodland animals, they have broad fluffy pads to keep their movement very silent: "Quiet as the winter, hidden as the new moon," the saying goes. Beautiful creatures. Such a shame to kill them.

"Good God!" I exclaim to David, unable to contain my horror. "It says here that you are permitted to shoot muskoxen on the Seward Peninsula. That's terrible. The poor creatures are practically extinct."

"Ain't nobody but Eskimos live on that part of Seward Peninsula and I imagine they've been hunting muskoxen for the last fifteen thousand years. Big-game hunters will pay a small fortune to hunt a muskox, so it is an important source of income for the native people who act as guides and outfitters."

I can tell that it will do no good to argue about this, so I consult my map of Alaska to locate the Seward Peninsula, the most western extent of Alaska. This is the exact area that Lillian would have had to traverse in order to get to Siberia. It sets me to reconsidering her fate.

"What do you reckon Lillian's chances of survival might have been? Let's suppose she ditched her boat and went back to travelling overland. Do you think she could have survived?"

"Very much doubt it. You know, this country is littered with the bones of people who've died out here that no one knows about. Search parties go looking for one body and are just as likely to find others they can't identify. They could be from the stampede, they could be Russians or they could have died quite recently. Rarely do you get intact skeletons, because the animals have gnawed the bones and scattered them."

"That's why it took so long to twig to the cannibalism on the Franklin expedition," I chip in eagerly. "For many years people saw the broken scatter of bones around the campsite at Booth Point as the work of animals. Now we know it wasn't simply that."

"Uh-huh." David gives me a disconcerted look and continues his narrative. "I remember hearing about the skeleton of a woman found in a burnt-out cabin near Fairbanks a few years back. She was Caucasian, in her mid-thirties and had been shot in the head. The forensic evidence built up a detailed profile that did not match any reported missing persons. Nor could they match her extensive dental work.

To this day they don't know who she was. That woman could just be your Lillian."

"Putting homicide to one side for the moment, is it possible that she could have survived? It was the summer and there would have been food about."

"Only if she was a skilled hunter and knew what she was looking to eat. Otherwise she'd end up like Chris McCandless."

"Who is he?"

"You haven't heard about him? Crazy young guy walked into the Denali National Park a year or so back, intending to live off the land. Wanted to *find himself* in the wilderness." David momentarily takes his hands off the wheel to make quotation marks in the air. "A bunch of moose hunters found his dead body four months later. Died of starvation in the middle of summer, only forty kilometres from the town of Healy. He took photographs of himself and wrote a diary, but it took a real long while to find out his true identity. There's a book about him called *Into the Wild.*" His left arm reaches across to the glovebox and extracts a battered paperback. "You can borrow my copy. It's a great read."

"These narratives of starvation absolutely fascinate me."

"There's many more. When I was a kid there was some hippie built himself a cabin on the Black River just northwest of here so he could commune with nature. A ranger found his gear, including two rifles and camping equipment, in the empty cabin, wide open to the elements and filled with snow."

"What happened to him?"

"He was never found. There is always some fruit loop wandering off into the wilderness to find himself. Notice I say 'himself.' Lillian is the first woman I've ever heard of. You think that was what she was doing, trying to find herself?"

"I doubt that she had read David Thoreau. It isn't really part of Jewish spirituality, is it, to test oneself in the wilderness? It's a Christian thing, I think, following Jesus's example of fasting for forty days and forty nights in the desert."

"Wait up. Wasn't Jesus a Jew? Maybe it is a Hebrew tradition."

"Lillian was at it for a good deal longer than forty days and nights. And why would she keep on going? I'm beginning to think of her as an extraordinarily peripatetic bag lady. Perpetually moving on for no rational reason; just some crazy compulsion to perambulate. Only I don't know where she ended up."

"She drowned." David sounds definite. "Body taken by the bears. This is no country for anyone who doesn't know how to look out for themselves."

"I'm very reluctant to give in to such a mundane conclusion," I say stubbornly.

"Got a better explanation?"

"You know I haven't."

We are making such good time that David decides to stop to allow me to spot a moose, as I have yet to see one. He pulls off at a place overlooking a broad plain and we climb out, eager to stretch our legs. David hands me a pair of high-powered binoculars, and I scan the softly glowing, rust-coloured landscape for the telltale sign of the sun glinting on antlers. This is perfect moose country, he tells me. Originally, it would have been spruce forest, but over many centuries it has been burned by the Athapaskan people to create moose habitat.

Now it is colonized by fireweed, which gives the terrain its gorgeous ruddy tints.

Every few minutes a pickup truck drives by and hoots the horn or flashes the lights, which I suspect is hunter code for "Have you seen one?" But I can't see one and the blackflies are flying up my trouser legs, swarming around my face and invading my ears. I could easily be persuaded there were no moose left in the far Northwest.

Driving toward Tok, I count thirty more hunters' vehicles parked beside the road. Many have wives standing guard beside the empty pickup, gun in hand. We pass one woman on her knees, probably praying that her husband can bag them a moose. America is a deeply religious country.

After the superb majesty of the landscape, I am quite un-prepared for the shambles that is the town of Tok, a hideous stretch of garish gift shops, shabby motels and frumpish supermarkets, all shouting their offerings in a multitude of gaudy signs.

David drops me at the information centre, where I can find a convenient place to stay and confirm that the bus to Haines will pick me up the following morning. He comes in with me to carry my pack and make sure I am well looked after. We help ourselves to a polystyrene cup of coffee—unspeakably vile—while I write out for him contacts at uni-versities in Australia, my home phone number and my e-mail address. He promises to visit, if not next year, then in the year of the Olympics.

With a powerful sense of loss, I watch his long, lean frame amble back to his dusty Toyota and drive away toward the apartment in Anchorage with the freezer of bear meat.

Looking about me, I notice the stuffed body of a huge grizzly at the other end of the building, rearing up on its hind legs and looking suitably ferocious. On close inspection, I decide that it is a good three metres high and has claws at least ten centimetres long.

Equally awestruck are the elderly couple who stand on the other side of the animal, wearing the sexless and shapeless uniform of senior American tourists. The squat husband is dressed in a T-shirt and blue nylon jacket with matching baseball cap and running shoes. His wife, with tightly curled, carroty hair, is a head taller and wears the same jacket, T-shirt and shoes, but she also has a money pouch clamped round her hips. I presume theirs is the RV I can see parked outside.

"Can you imagine that men could hunt this fellow with bow and arrows?" I ask.

The husband takes off his glasses, wipes them and puts them back on to better scrutinize the beast.

"Bow and arrows," he repeats. "I'll be damned."

Proxy Hunting

At first light the pungent smell of slightly rank meat assails me when I open the door of my motel room to a crisp Alaskan morning. A pickup truck with fresh moose antlers is parked directly outside, just one of eight pickups along the length of the motel. As I walk past the line of trucks I am distressed to see more sets of antlers, and grimace at the thought of what is packed under the tarpaulins in the back.

It is only six o'clock, yet the motel café is already packed with jovial hunters, leaving no spare table for my breakfast. I bristle at the sight of them, but immediately they vacate a table for me and include me in their quick repartee with the same easy grace as David. I am utterly disarmed by their inclusiveness and thoroughly entertained by their infectious banter. It is not possible to hold fast to my disapproval in the company of men who are so unaffectedly courteous and so unabashedly happy.

Two of these blokes are from Juneau, it turns out, and they will be taking the ferry from Haines. The offer of a lift is inevitable, but I blanch at the idea of driving all that way wedged between exuberant men with the butchered carcasses of moose just behind my back. I quickly reassure them that I have already bought my ticket and am looking forward to the bus trip. They don't seem too disappointed at having to forgo my company.

The half-empty bus allows me a seat to myself, near the front with a big picture window to enjoy the spectacular scenery. Here the trembling aspen along the roadside still hold their shimmering canary-coloured leaves. Towering above them are the white points of the great St. Elias Range, touched with a soft blush of the rising sun. I feel a thrill run through my body from my toes to my scalp. I have missed the high mountain peaks. The forbidding rock faces and the sharp points thrusting into the sky are what most attracts me to the Far North, so unlike anything in my own worn-down and ancient landscape. As the mountains come into full view, the grizzled and taciturn man sitting across the aisle, who has hitherto responded to my friendly overtures with "yup" or "nope," suddenly grows communicative.

"Them mountains look like somebody took to 'em with a paintbrush, eh?"

For the rest of the journey he never says another word.

This astonishing terrain is still making itself. Unlike Beringia, this is a glaciated landscape that was covered by ice until ten thousand years ago. When the climate warmed, the receding glaciers created an expanse of grasslands between the mountain ranges, inducing grazing animals and the ancestors of the Southern Tuchone Nations to move in from Beringia.

At one point, the bus runs alongside Kluane Lake, which is smooth as glass, throwing back a perfect reflection of the mountains that spring straight up from the water's edge. I see on my map that the roseate peaks captured in the lake are aptly named the Ruby Range.

I am travelling along the northern boundary of the Wrangell, St. Elias and Kluane wilderness. At the heart of this fantastic and huge World Heritage Area, which straddles both sides of the U.S.-Canadian border, is the Kaskawulsh Glacier, shown in photographs as a monumental zigzag of striated ice sweeping through the mountains.

Glaciers are remarkable to me because I live on a dry and arid continent. A booklet on the World Heritage Area explains that glaciers form when more snow falls than melts, and this is crystallized into ice grains, which are pressed into a solid, airless mass of a pure aqua colour. Eventually gravity pulls the glacier downhill like a sluggish river, churning the earth as it goes. This phenomenon is called "surging." Most glaciers, including the Kaskawulsh, are in retreat. On the other side of the St. Elias Range, the Bering Glacier began surging in 1995 and moved six kilometres in as many weeks.

It would be exciting to see such a thing.

It certainly was thrilling to see a chunk break off from a glacier, as happened once when I had hiked alone up to the Plain of Six Glaciers in the Rocky Mountains. I was eating my solitary lunch on a bed of shale by the tongue of the Victoria Glacier when a huge thunderclap caused me to jerk my head around in time to see a big chunk break off the lip of the glacier and rumble down toward Lake Louise in the valley far below. Ten minutes later, an even louder crack heralded another glacier segment thundering down the mountainside. Though it was a good kilometre distant, the sound and spectacle took my breath away.

At Haines Junction, the bus stops for a meal break.

I feel a tug of nostalgia for this unprepossessing town. I've been here before, six or seven years ago, when Michael and I rafted down that mother of wild rivers, the mighty Tatshenshini. My heart skipped a beat more than once on that particular trip.

For all that Haines Junction boasts of being the gateway to the Kluane wilderness, it is shabby and unloved, split down the middle by the macadam of the Al-Can Highway. The town's one gesture to civic pride is a bizarre concrete structure, shaped like an inverted cone and painted to resemble a dung-brown mountain extruding various species of wildlife: a moose, a bear and a Dall sheep. Windblown debris has collected around its base.

The drivers change at Haines Junction and the new man in charge is much more loquacious, giving his opinion over the loudspeaker about the American president's sexual peccadillos and the disadvantages of NAFTA. He also acts as a tourist guide, pointing out the wildlife that our less experienced eyes might miss: a wolf slinking into the undergrowth beside the road, bald eagles soaring on the wind currents, and white dots high on a mountain ledge that he claims are Dall sheep. If we were passing in the rutting season, he explains, we would be able to hear the clash of the sheep's great horns echoing around the mountains.

In the early evening the bus carries me through the majesty of the Chilkat Pass, where the chiselled facets of the mountains resemble a painter's palette of mauve, sienna, russet, charcoal and celadon. On the other side of the pass, a distinct change is noticeable as we descend into a coastal rain forest of huge spruce trees, the rich green marred by stands of dead spars. The spruce has come under attack from an infestation of beetle, the bus driver announces, reassuring his passengers that these infestations are cyclical and will cause no long-term damage.

"What goes around comes around," he tells us philosophically.

Haines, Alaska, hunkers down beneath the St. Elias Range at the very tip of the Lynn Canal, quite close to where the stampede tent city of Dyea used to be. No matter how gimcrack and unplanned, Haines could not fail to be stunning with a natural setting hard to better anywhere in the world. Tonight the whole town is illuminated by a huge tourist cruise ship, ablaze with lights like a gigantic Christmas decoration.

Even the dazzle of the cruise ship in the harbour cannot diminish the brilliant night sky: a velvety midnight blue with the pearly splash of the Milky Way overhead and hundreds of scintillating stars. The northern skies never appear as brilliant as my own night skies in southern Tasmania, but this is the best sky I've yet seen in the Northern Hemisphere.

I should be grateful to the tricky Raven for this nighttime splendour.

In the beginning, there was no moon or stars. Raven learned of a powerful chief living on the banks of the Nass River whose daughter possessed the moon and the stars in a carved cedar box. Raven flew across to the Nass and settled in a tall tree, where he turned himself into a hemlock needle that fell into the daughter's drinking cup as she drank. Inside the daughter, Raven developed into a baby and was born to be the chief's dearly loved first grandson. In pride of place in the centre of the house sat the chest that Raven coveted. He demanded to play with its contents and wouldn't stop crying until his grandfather gave them to him. As soon as he had them, Raven threw them up through the smokehole and they scattered across the sky.

Where they remain to this night.

My Alaskan hostess is beside herself with pleasure at the stars, exclaiming over and over about the sky. This is the first clear night for three months, the best starlit sky in years, she reports, seeking confirmation from her other guest, a man in his mid-thirties with a rather plain face and short-cropped ginger hair who is reading in the glass atrium, where tomorrow's breakfast will be served.

Lewis is an ex-marine officer from "back east" who has come to Alaska to do some hunting. He will not be joining me for an early breakfast, he explains, because he will be on his way before dawn to paddle across the mouth of the near-freezing Lynn Canal in a canoe. His intention is to climb the wild shore opposite, right up above the treeline, to set up camp. Then he is determined to stalk and hunt a mountain goat. If he succeeds, he will have to bone out the animal, then carry all the meat, skin and horns on his back, down to his canoe, and paddle across the canal once again.

When I ask if he hunts with bow and arrows, I am fairly confident of the answer.

"There is no better way."

Lewis is an interesting fellow who rather confounds my stereotypes about both American marines and hunters. He is full of scorn for the moose hunters with their ATVs and their rifles with telescopic sights. The only decent way to hunt is the way it has been done since time immemorial.

"Don't you worry about the bears?" I ask.

"I've never had a problem with bears. I make it my business to stay downwind of them. Once I came face to face with a brown bear—that's a grizzly—picking berries. I just stared him down. After a while the bear dropped onto its four paws and lolloped away. They are magnificent, intelligent creatures. I'd never have it in me to kill one."

"They have it in them to kill you."

"Oh, sure. I did have one close shave with a grizzly up in the Brooks Range. This big male just came barrelling down the trail at me and I had no time to do anything but throw myself over the embankment. Luck was with me and the bear just kept right on going. I sprained my arm and was in a lot of pain for a while, but no real damage was done."

"I have read that you can commune with bears, soul to soul."

"You wanna believe it. Native people, you know, always show respect to a creature as awesome as a grizzly. There's an old Indian story about a woman who was disrespectful about bears and later was forced to marry a bear to atone. Of course the bear turned into a handsome young brave once she understood the error of her ways."

"A Native American version of *Beauty and the Beast*," I say. "There is a similar variant in Borneo among the Iban, who tell many stories about women who marry orangutans."

"Indigenous people have been around for tens of thousands of years. It is blind stupidity not to pay attention to the way they see the universe." Lewis stands up and extends his hand in courtesy. "Well, Cassandra, it has been just grand talking with you. Now I need my sleep."

When I enter the kitchen to get some milk for my coffee, I ask my hostess about her other guest. As she understands it, Lewis did a tour of duty in Bosnia and has been deeply scarred by the experience. He has been coming to Alaska every year since he left the army.

"Such a nice man," she reflects. "I get the feeling, though, that he is only really 'together' when he is alone in the wilderness."

I am beginning to perceive this as a common pattern.

Lost in the Wild

The road to the Alaska ferry wharf runs northeast of Haines and skirts a river boiling with salmon in a frenzy of sexual congress.

These are pink salmon, the taxi driver tells me, and she switches off her meter to allow us both to get out and make a close observation. The fish are in the process of changing, which has made them a mottled puce colour rather than a brilliant crimson, and the males are transformed into something utterly grotesque. Crouching on my haunches for a closer inspection, I feel the pressure of the driver's hand on my shoulder and look up to see a big grizzly coming into the river to feed, followed by two playful cubs.

In next to no time, we are at the centre of a traffic jam of cars and buses that have stopped to view the spectacle. For about ten minutes, mother bear pays no attention to the excited whispering from the bank, then she suddenly levels a quizzical look at the assembled throng and bounds into a thicket of golden dwarf willow, her cubs in quick pursuit.

All the vehicles start up at once, so we now travel to the

wharf in slow procession, bumper to bumper, which is almost guaranteed to delay the ferry sailing. I am relieved to see that the taxi driver has left her meter switched off. There is already a very long line of cars and pickups waiting to board the ferry, all of them large four-wheel drives and many with moose antlers strapped to the roof.

I grieve for the male moose population of southeastern Alaska. With a hunting season that runs between fourteen days and a month, there can't be that many more of them left standing.

Once the ferry begins to move down the narrow Lynn Canal, steep hills press in on either side. A dense carpet of spruce runs straight up from the waterline, broken occasionally by the silver threads of glacial cascades, which deposit a ribbon of aqua on top of the dense blue-green water of the canal.

I have found a deliciously sunny spot on the perimeter of the open solarium deck where the backpackers set up camp, and have commandeered a plastic chair. Sheltered from the wind, I settle down to read David's copy of *Into the Wild*.

Jon Krakauer's story of the death of Chris McCandless is beautifully done: a compelling account of a young man from an affluent suburb of Washington, D.C., intellectually gifted and an elite athlete, who suddenly gave away the entire balance of his $24,000 savings account, abandoned all his possessions, changed his name and created a new life for himself wandering across North America in search of transcendent experiences. For two years his close and supportive family had no idea what had happened to him, until his emaciated remains were finally identified in a Fairbanks morgue, weeks after his partly decomposed body was found in a bus on the edge of the Denali National Park early in September 1992.

Paul Gallien was able to identify the body. He remembered having given a lift to a twenty-four-year-old man calling himself Alex who asked to be dropped at the edge of the Denali park, saying he intended to walk deep into the bush and live off the land. He had noticed that the young man's backpack looked as if it weighed only about twenty pounds, an improbably light load for a stay of several months in the backcountry, and his gear was exceedingly minimal for the harsh conditions of the interior. He had only a .22 rifle, with a bore too small to kill large game, which he would have to do if he hoped to remain very long in the backcountry, and he had no axe, no compass, no detailed map of the area. His passenger admitted that the only food in his backpack was a five kilogram bag of rice. Gallien had offered to take him back to Anchorage to buy him some decent gear, then drive him wherever he wanted to go, but he was rebuffed. When asked if he had a hunting licence, Alex had replied, "How I feed myself is none of the government's business. Fuck their stupid rules." He insisted on giving Gallien what little money he possessed and his watch. "I don't want to know what the time is. I don't want to know what day it is or where I am. None of that matters," he explained. That was on 28 April 1992, a little over four months before his body was found.

From the evidence pieced together by the state troopers, and later by Krakauer, it is apparent that McCandless followed a disused dirt road called the Stampede Trail, which ran for about seventy kilometres into the backcountry, just north of the town of Healy. About halfway along the trail, there was an old abandoned bus from the 1940s that had served as a backcountry shelter for hunters and trappers. It was there that McCandless had lived and died between April and September 1992. Ironically, the wilderness where Mc-Candless was determined to become "lost in the wild" was only about twenty-five kilometres from the main road into the Denali National Park. Scattered within a ten-kilometre radius of the bus were four well-stocked cabins. Had he known this and had he been carrying a detailed survey map, it might have saved his life.

From the writings found in the bus, it was apparent that McCandless was greatly influenced by Jack London. Not long after arriving at the bus, he scrawled on a sheet of ply-wood an exultant declaration of independence:

> Now after two rambling years comes the final and great-est adventure: the climactic battle to kill the false being within and victoriously conclude the spiritual revolution. Ten days and nights of freight trains and hitch-hiking bring him to the Great White North. No longer to be poisoned by civilisation he flees, and walks alone upon the land to become *lost in the wild*.

As this credo reveals, the young man was following a minor American tradition of taking one's wounded soul to the wilderness for a cure, a fairly harmless self-indulgence in the woods of Michigan or Maine, but never in the vast, un-peopled and savage wilderness of Alaska. To walk into the subarctic wilderness without proper equipment or a map, or any decent all-weather gear, is not simply foolhardy; it is an act of supreme hubris. Krakauer, who has more than a sneak-ing admiration for him, admits that McCandless had gran-diose spiritual ambitions when he ambled totally unprepared into the wilderness to discover the inner working of his soul. The young man quickly discovered that the more powerful imperatives were those of the body: his diary entries are almost entirely about food.

These sparse entries allow Krakauer to determine that although McCandless was severely weakened by malnutrition and his body probably began to consume itself, his actual death was caused by food he ate. Krakauer supposes that McCandless unwittingly ate wild potato seeds that can have a toxin known to inhibit the body's capacity to turn food into usable energy, thus rapidly hastening the process of starvation. Krakauer tells us that one of McCandless's last acts was to take a photograph of himself with his little camera:

> Standing near the bus under the high Alaska sky, one hand holding his final note toward the camera lens, the other raised in a brave, beatific farewell. His face is horribly emaciated, almost skeletal. But if he pitied himself in those last difficult hours—because he was so young, because he was alone, because his body had betrayed him and his will let him down—it is not apparent from the photograph. He is smiling in the picture, and there is no mistaking the look in his eyes: Chris McCandless was at peace, serene as a monk gone to God.

So engrossing is Krakauer's narrative that I almost miss a pod of orca whales alongside the ferry, the sun shining on their glossy blue-black dorsal fins as they slice through the water, leaving silver streaks in their wake. They frolic like dolphins, blowing clouds of misty vapour high in the air, diving and surfacing, with the water cascading off their magnificent tails just like Niagara Falls.

I see that the surrounding landscape is heart-stopping now that the ferry has entered the Inside Passage. On my left-hand side, a massive saw-toothed mountain range pierces the washed-out sky, and the sun radiates off the alabaster planes of the massive Juneau icefield. Between the ferry and the shore lies a tiny island on which sit several whitewashed buildings with bright red roofs, probably Russian in origin, marking the entrance to the narrow channel which runs into the capital city of Juneau. All this beauty is perfectly reflected in the water, which is as still as a millpond.

At Juneau I watch a steady stream of pickups sprout ATVs and antlers as most of the mooseketeers take their leave.

"Look at all those timid public servants going home with their trophies to prove that they are really frontiersmen."

Turning around, I locate the scornful voice and see that it belongs to a bearded and weather-beaten man in his late twenties, who looks like he probably is a frontiersman.

"Not impressed with all that slaughter?" I ask him.

"Ha." He makes a dismissive gesture. "Those guys are perfect arseholes. They don't need the meat; they are just desperate to kill something bigger and better than they are."

I grin broadly to show my appreciation.

"See you're reading *Into the Wild*," he continues. "What do you think about that guy McCandless?"

I say I am struck by the terrible hubris in one so young and intelligent.

It transpires that this man runs adventure tours and rafting excursions in Denali, and knows that country very well; he knows exactly where McCandless died. He points out, much as Jon Krakauer has done, that the boy might have been a greenhorn, but he had achieved something quite remarkable to survive for sixteen weeks living completely off the land.

"I know I couldn't do it and nor could most of those people who call McCandless a fool," he tells me. "If he had not made a couple of mistakes he would have survived."

"Surely the Alaskan wilderness is not a place that will permit a couple of mistakes. He had insufficient awe. He thought his will could triumph over anything."

"I don't see it that way."

"Hubris," I repeat.

"Plenty of people will disagree with you," he says, wandering off to his encampment in the solarium.

Nearly everyone on this ferry seems to have read Krakauer's book and to have an opinion about it. Later in the day, when I have followed the sun to another part of the ship, my reading is interrupted again by a couple of young backpackers who want to know what I think about the book.

This time I am more cautious about my opinion and reverse the question.

The boy is very keen to explain what a cool dude McCandless was. These two have walked the Stampede Trail in his footsteps. Been to the bus and seen the sad detritus he left behind.

"It's all just as Chris left it," his girlfriend chimes in. "Nothing has been taken."

I am astounded by this revelation. "You mean to tell me that people make a special trip to the bus. For what, to pay homage?"

"Sure," the boy says happily. "Every summer people make a pilgrimage to the bus."

Shortly after the conversation with the backpackers, I am interrupted yet again by a lovely young German who tells me her name is Elsa. She has been travelling around Alaska on a bike with her dog. The pooch travels on a little cart at the back. She tells me she is studying at the university in Düsseldorf and that she and her dog flew directly from Düsseldorf to Anchorage.

Elsa is on her way home, but she will come back next year to get a cabin deep in the woods and spend the winter, she explains. Just her and the dog in the wilderness. Elsa has also read *Into the Wild*. She even tried to ride her bike down the Stampede Trail to the bus. It is a source of great disappointment to her that the trail was too wet and she could not make it. She told me that she had spoken to plenty of others who managed to visit the bus, maybe twenty or thirty people, and that the bus was exactly as Krakauer described it.

When I wonder aloud why no one has taken souvenirs, her pretty face registers a look of horror.

"Oh no," she says earnestly. "If you have struggled down that trail and managed to get to the bus, you would not take anything away. It would be disrespectful."

"Obviously you think that McCandless was a special kind of person."

"Of course." Elsa is adamant. "I come back in April next year to go to the bus. I must pay my respects."

Excusing myself from this earnest conversation, I walk away from Elsa to the cafeteria in a state of astonishment.

The Vision Quest

The waterfront at Ketchikan, Alaska, is built on timber pilings over the sea, while steep wooden staircases lead up to three rows of houses on the bluff above. It is a tiny town, squeezed between the mountains and a narrow arm of the Inside Passage. The name Ketchikan is said to be Tlingit for

Salmon Creek, which is doubtless the case, since the creek on which the town is built is awash with spent salmon. The pervasive odour of decaying fish is part of its ambience at this time of the year.

I have alighted from the ferry on a whim to take potluck in Ketchikan. As it happens, my potluck has been remarkably good.

It is a peerless day. Unusual. It rains here, buckets down more often than not. At a rickety little café in the picturesque historic section of town, built on timber pilings over the malodorous Salmon Creek, I enjoy fresh barbecued salmon and a cold beer. The sunshine is warm enough to burn my exposed arms. All the frenetic activity caused by two huge cruise ships is confined to the waterfront itself, a continuous line of gift shops selling extremely expensive goods, including, I notice with some dismay, soft woollen scarves made from muskox hair.

I have chosen this quaint, sheltered corner, despite the whiff of decaying salmon, because it has a view over the water, and I am mesmerized by a group of kayakers crossing the narrows with the sun at their backs. Like semaphore, the sunlight flashes each time they raise their paddles from the water.

Already I have discovered one of the best small bookshops in North America, run by a marvellous woman in her seventies known to one and all as Miz Lillian. Her close-packed shop has four crowded shelves of poetry, and the biggest section is devoted to feminist books. Miz Lillian herself is a feisty feminist, who puts me in mind of my own remarkable mother, a pioneer of the women's liberation movement in Australia. Miz Lillian came to Alaska quite by chance fifty-one years ago, fell in love with it and stayed on in Ketchikan. So she told me.

Luxuriating in the soft sunshine, I speculate that my Lillian could possibly have done something similar. She may not have drowned. She may have ditched her flimsy craft and made it overland to a remote and tiny Alaskan outpost like Woodchopper, where she would have been just one more eccentric loner. She may have stayed on to become just another Miz Lillian, of no interest to those "from Outside."

It is as good a story as any.

As the kayakers round the narrows out of sight, I settle down to read the diary of Sophia Cracroft, niece to Sir John Franklin and companion to Lady Jane. The book details the year she and Lady Jane spent in the town of Sitka in the Inside Passage in 1870, waiting in vain for the recovery of relics from Sir John's tragic voyage. Her ladyship found Sitka distasteful because of the impositions of her landlord, who was a mere butcher and, worse yet, a German Jew. For her part, Miss Cracroft was much disturbed by the Tlingit Indians, with whom she haggled relentlessly over the carved items they offered for sale. The "wretched creatures," with their painted faces and weird keening, made her uneasy, and she willingly accepted the stories that the Indians made a ritual sacrifice of their slaves. Just as disagreeable were the ubiquitous ravens, of which, she complained, there were a great many, of great size, very impudent and disagreeably noisy.

Raven is a potent presence here in Ketchikan. A stunning black-and-red poster of Raven in glossy glory bursting from a steaming cup is all over the town, advertising Raven's Brew coffee with the boast that it is the last legal high in Alaska. I order a cup to finish my meal; this seems fitting, as I am all but surrounded by bright-eyed fellows who peck and caw among the carcasses of Salmon Creek, the purple sheen of their black feathers iridescent in the bright sunlight.

By the time I have savoured the excellent coffee, I am thoroughly bored with Miss Cracroft's pretensions and decide to take a walk about the town. Passing an Internet café, I remember my earlier search for Lillian on the Social Security Death Index, available on the World Wide Web.

Locating this site one more time, I find a possible fit for my imagined Alaskan narrative: Lillian Smith, born in 1897. That is just the right age for my quarry. I reason to myself that Smith would be the most obvious name to adopt if no one could get their tongue around her proper name. Lillian Smith died in Sitka, a small island in the Inside Passage, in 1979. Sitka is a considerable distance from Dawson City. As the crow flies, it is about thirteen hundred kilometres away. Interestingly, though, her last Social Security benefit was paid in Skagway, that stunningly beautiful place at the head of the Lynn Canal, which is also the most accessible Alaskan town to the south of Dawson City.

It could be.

At a stretch.

Searching on variations of the name Olejnik, I turn up another tantalizing possibility in Lillian Aleinikoff, who died in a nursing home in Florida only three years ago. She is just the right age, having been born in 1896. This prospect really tickles me. It is fun to think that Lillian made a pile from prospecting abandoned mine claims at the top of the world and became rich enough to retire to the perpetual sun of Florida, where she lived to be nearly a hundred years old.

My walk eventually takes me to the Tlingit village of Saxman, about five kilometres south of Ketchikan. Here I discover an impressive collection of elaborately carved, brightly decorated totems. Like all First Nations of the Inside Passage, the Tlingit built impressive rectangular log houses with richly carved interior posts; they turned the massive tree trunks into complex narratives of their various clan totems. The raven figures prominently, together with the bear, the eagle and the wolf. Returning, I observe another mighty cruise ship, at least six storeys high and the length of two city blocks, tying up at the wharf. It is throwing a shadow across the entire town. In high summer there are usually five such ships a day. This floating monstrosity is the last boat of the season.

I can already feel a tangible sense of release about the town.

There is certainly no shortage of places for the locals to let their hair down. I pass a multitude of narrow, darkened saloon bars, as many as two or three to a block. Each time, I shoot a surreptitious glance into the dingy interior and catch the flicker of a cable sports channel on the television and the hunched outline of a man absorbed in the game.

I'm thirsty, but these are not my kind of places.

The B&B I have chosen for the night is a timber house on three levels, cut into the steep bluff at the very extremity of Ketchikan, with primordial forest at its back door. I have quite a climb to reach it, but I am rewarded by a spectacular view over the Inside Passage. Near the bottom of the steep wooden steps up to the entrance is a very large cage on wheels, rather like those used to transport circus animals, from which a disgusting smell is wafting into the sweet evening air.

My hosts are sitting on the steps, high enough above the town to escape the shadow of the cruise ships, drinking Fosters Lager in the last of the day's sunshine. Matt is an Australian who runs kayaking adventure tours with his English wife, Jane. It was their kayak group I saw crossing the narrows earlier in the day.

Noticing me wrinkle my nose when I pass the cage, Matt tells me that this is a trap for the foraging bear that lives behind their house.

"Fat lot of good it will do," he says with a laugh. "Pat the bear is way too smart to be caught in a trap."

"I can't imagine how it got here," Jane adds, making room for me on the steps. "We didn't request it. We like old Pat."

"But how come the bear's here at all?" I ask. "In the tourist brochure it says that all the bears have been removed from the communities of the Inside Passage because they had become habituated to garbage."

Jane confirms that this is true and that it was a very expensive operation to trap all the black bears and fly them to an offshore island. "What they seem to have forgotten is that bears can swim. A number of them just came right back so they could continue to get their toothpaste fix."

On the sunny steps, gazing out over a myriad of fiords and islands, I find it is easy enough to ignore the odour from the bear trap. Jane identifies Gravina as the closest large island, with Annette Island to the southwest. As the last of the sun slips behind the ragged outline of Gravina Island, my thoughts turn to dinner.

"Where is a good place to eat in Ketchikan?"

"Juneau," says Matt without a moment's hesitation. "You must eat with us," he adds, in response to my crestfallen look.

"We have bottles of good Aussie red and will just throw another shrimp on the barbie."

"Be warned. I might dissolve into a flood of homesick tears."

"Are you coming or going?" Jane inquires.

"Tomorrow I'll get the ferry to Prince Rupert, then fly to Vancouver for a connecting flight home."

"Half your luck," Matt retorts, rather to my surprise.

"Surely you wouldn't be homesick in such a spectacular place as this." My arm sweeps across the vista of water and islands below us.

"I couldn't settle anywhere outside Australia except for the Alaska panhandle," he explains. "But by Christ it rains. And they don't have universal health coverage."

"How do you manage for health insurance?"

A look of private amusement flits between Matt and Jane.

"We just keep our fingers crossed," she says.

Dinner is a riotous and very Australian affair. Many bottles of full-bodied Australian red wine are consumed. Under some pressure from Jane, Matt takes out his guitar. It turns out he used to sing professionally with a well-known folk band. He is also something of an ethnologist and has collected folk songs from all over the Americas.

Tonight he sings of Australia:

For the rain never falls on the dusty Diamantina.

Songs of the parched and empty outback set me wondering out loud about the story of Chris McCandless.

Matt and Jane have both read *Into the Wild*—I swear everyone in Alaska must have read this book—and Matt puts an interesting spin on it. In his view, McCandless's need to go into the wild stemmed from a residual culture of

Native Americans. Despite the terrible frontier conflict, he reckons that Americans have absorbed elements of Indian culture and spirituality in a way that has never happened in Australia.

"I'm no expert on this, but I have always thought that this business of taking to the wilderness to find spiritual awakening is derived from the vision quest of the Plains Indians."

Jane and I both look at him in bewilderment.

"What I am talking about is a young man's rite of passage, when he goes up a mountain or some other lonely spot, fasts and performs other feats of endurance, and waits for a spirit to make itself known. This spirit becomes a sort of alter ego, guide, helper or 'familiar' for the rest of his life, appearing and helping in times of crisis."

"So that's what McCandless was up to when he walked into the Denali National Park?" I say.

"Without being conscious of it, yes. He was probably seeking his guiding spirit. The Mexican concept of the *nahual*, or double, is similar. My guess is the quest was once much more widespread across North America and has just seeped into the American psyche."

"You are right about it being an American thing," Jane interjects with a laugh. "I mean, can you imagine some Aussie bloke walking into the Great Sandy Desert to find himself?"*

---

*By a weird coincidence, almost two years after this conversation, a thirty-three-year-old fireman from Fairbanks, Alaska, named Robert Bogucki, cycled into the Australian Great Sandy Desert in search of spiritual enlightenment. According to his father, Bogucki wanted to utilize "the vast privateness" of the desert in an effort to be alone with God. After being given up for dead, he was found forty-two days later, weak and emaciated but still carrying a water bottle, a compass and a

Nothing Else Matters

My head is swirling when I am dragged out of sleep by a thumping on the door of my room at the bottom of Matt and Jane's house.

I wonder who could possibly be at the door at this hour. The illuminated clock beside my bed tells me it is 4:00 a.m. Without switching on the light, I tiptoe over to the window near the door. When I tweak the heavy drapes, I find myself face to face with a large black bear. A most disgruntled-looking bear. He can't see me, I realize, once my initial terror has subsided. He is too busy trying to open the new bear-proof garbage bin. As I watch him clamber over the stair rail into the garden of the house next door, I can hear the blood pounding in my temples. I am in such a state of alarm that I would not have been able to communicate with the soul of that bear even if it had occurred to me to try.

Back in the tangled sheets of the unfamiliar bed, my body refuses to relax into slumber. I am at the very end of my tether. I can't take this any more. Too many nights have been spent in strange beds on this wild-goose chase after Lillian. She remains as elusive and enigmatic as when the trip began. I toss and turn for a few more hours, wrestling with disappointment. It is a huge relief to finally see a sharp sliver of sunlight thrusting through the crack in the window drapes.

---

return airline ticket to Alaska. Bogucki's transcendental itch was something that Australians were not able to appreciate. Following his rescue, estimated to have cost $40,000, he was puzzled and hurt to be inundated with abusive mail, some of which labelled him "a complete fuckwit."

Thank the Lord I am going home today.

At breakfast Jane is amused by the story of my nocturnal encounter with the bear, having neglected to warn me that Pat is a regular visitor.

"Thank goodness you didn't open the door," she says merrily.

Being mauled by a disgruntled black bear is probably worth millions of dollars in compensation. I think it best not to ask whether their public liability insurance is of the same order as their health insurance.

"You had more than one visitation," Jane continues. "A fax came for you in the night."

My husband is the only person who knows I am here. I snatch at the fax in terror that it's bad news. Anxiety turns to bemusement when I see that Michael has forwarded a sheaf of pages related to research on Lillian, of absolutely no use to me now. I fold them up and shove them into my shoulder bag, my eyes misty from the simple message he has scrawled on the cover sheet: "I'll be at Sydney airport to meet you, lovely one. With bells on."

Strapped into my window seat above the vast Pacific Ocean, I do my best to make the time pass. It is an exhausting trip, and it always seems longer because we gain a day in crossing the International Date Line.

I put my seat back, take a pill, pull the eyeshade down and will myself to sleep.

Waking into breaking daylight and the offer of fruit juice, I rummage in my shoulder bag for one of those little sachets infused with cologne I keep for such early mornings on long-distance flights, and I find the faxes Michael has forwarded to me.

When I take them out to read, I realize that one is actually a fax from Russia. It is not clear exactly where in Russia, as there is no identifying information on the fax header. It is from a Dr. Arkady Cherkasov from the International Northern Forum Academy, in response to one of my very early e-mails. He writes:

> One cannot *walk* from Alaska to Chukotka in any season, because of moving ice. From the shores of Chukotka, if one ever reaches them, one cannot *walk* to Siberia or anywhere at all, as there are no roads and no reason to walk inland: in spite of how it looks on the map, Chukotka is more of an island, and the only way to reach Siberia is to sail along the Pacific coast several thousand miles.
>
> In the period between 1929 and 1956, the Soviet Far East, and especially Chukotka, was a virtual KGB land, entirely under the control of the notorious gulag authorities. So, in Providenija or anywhere, people won't recollect anything but the atrocities of the Stalinist regime and the concentration camps. I doubt they have any archives at all. So if Lillian Alling's story is your main interest in your presumed trip to Chukotka, it is not worth it (by the way, I hear this name for the first time).

Dr. Cherkasov's missive makes me feel pretty good. What a relief to know that I would have been barking up the wrong tree to go to Chukotka. A failure of nerve on my part can now be reinterpreted as a prudent and correct course of action.

Thank you, Dr. Cherkasov, whoever you may be.

The other two pages of faxes have been sent to me by the Whitehorse museum and consist of cuttings from 1973 editions of a British Columbia newspaper called the *Province*. I run my eyes over the first one, to see that the newspaper has rehashed the same old flights of fancy about Lillian walking to Russia. I barely glance at the second page, until I realize that it is of a very different order. A retired Mountie named Greenfield has written to the *Province* to set the record straight.

With increasing excitement I read on:

It was in August 1927 that the Polish woman Lillian Ailing walked through the Bulkley Valley in Northern BC in her attempt to get to Telegraph Creek. She had come to North Dakota to marry a countryman boy friend there but he had departed before her arrival. She then walked through Alberta and BC via Jasper and Prince George and had reached Kispiox on the Yukon Telegraph line about 30 miles north of Hazelton, when BC Provincial Police Constable George Wyman received a phone call and he immediately went to Kispiox by car and picked her up and brought her to Hazelton.

He locked her up on a vagrancy charge. It was at this point that I came into the picture. Constable Wyman had to go out of town on an urgent matter and he asked me to do the gaol guard duty until his return. I happened to be in Hazelton on patrol duties and it was not infrequent that members of the RC mounted police were asked and readily gave necessary assistance to the provincial police. When she appeared before Justice of the Peace Grant she was sentenced to five days to be served in Oakalla prison farm. She was then escorted to Oakalla by police matron Constance Cox and after the five days had elapsed Lillian was released immediately. I believe she spent the winter of 1927–28 in Vancouver.

In 1928 Lillian walked through the Bulkley Valley again, this time by night and over the Yukon Telegraph line to Telegraph Creek, early in the summer. In the latter part of October 1928 I received a letter addressed to Policeman Greenfield, Hazelton, from Lillian. She wrote in poor English that she had not found her beloved in Telegraph Creek as he had departed before her arrival. She had, however, found and married a kind man there. She thanked me for delaying her a year from meeting her beloved. She said she could remember my name but couldn't recall the name of the other policeman.

The letter was addressed to Hazelton but was sent on to me at Kitiwanga where I had been transferred.

Lillian's effects consisted of a man's heavy cloth overcoat that hung to ankle length in which she slept. She carried an iron bar about 16 inches long for defence purposes. She had a landing card showing her arrival at New York early in 1927 and showing her to be Polish. Her name on the card was spelt Ailing. She wore a pair of men's eight inch top boots.

I know nothing further after her letter to me in 1928. Lillian was very much in need of a bath, maybe one would not have sufficed!

I stare at this belated communication with amazement.

At long last I have an eyewitness account of Lillian's encounter with the provincial police. I know that Greenfield is genuine, because I saw his name when I was searching in the British Columbia Archives for police records in the

Bulkley River district. The archives even held some of his papers. I had a brief look at them, but they were not from this period. What really delights me is that for the first time, I have been given a rational explanation for Lillian's trek: she was pursuing a mate. Of course she was! No other explanation could be comprehensible. Moreover, this is the first time I have read any eyewitness account of where she said she was going: Telegraph Creek. That sounds altogether more plausible than Siberia. This change of destination does not diminish the reason the police arrested her, as it would have been suicidal to walk through the Skeena Mountains at that time of the year.

I remain puzzled by what Greenfield says about Lillian's letter being sent to him from Telegraph Creek in late October 1928. By that stage, Lillian had been living in Dawson City for two or three weeks. The postal services were very good in the Yukon, but even if it took a while for the letter to reach Greenfield, it is still most likely to have been written from Dawson City. Certainly not Telegraph Creek. The small bit of tangible evidence I do have places Lillian on the trail north of Telegraph Creek in July.

Could she have written such a letter?

Lillian's spoken language would have been Yiddish, and she was most likely schooled in Hebrew. Neither of these written languages share the same alphabet as English, so writing in English would be difficult. However, I am convinced that Lillian was capable of writing a basic letter in English.

I read the letter again looking for clues.

Greenfield does say that her English was poor. Well yes, it would be. All the accounts say she did not speak good English. Most likely the letter did not make perfect sense. So Lillian may not have indicated where she was at the time of writing, and Greenfield inferred it was Telegraph Creek, not understanding that she had walked all the way to Dawson City. No one would dream that a woman could manage such a thing. Reading Greenfield's missive one more time, I decide it points very strongly to Lillian having taken up with a man in Dawson City.

That's it! An explanation to account for the lack of information about her whereabouts over the winter in 1928–29.

In the remote subarctic, a woman on her own was a subject of intense interest and scrutiny, but a woman with a man was not. To all intents and purposes, she was rendered invisible.

Greenfield's explanation is quite plausible.

What, then, am I to make of the eyewitness account of her pushing off in a boat down the Yukon River in early June 1929?

There's no doubt that Lillian left by herself and that she had no provisions to suggest any kind of long journey. Equally, there is little doubt that she did not get even as far down the river as Eagle, Alaska. I do not believe for a moment that she said she was going to Siberia. She didn't say it when she left Dawson City any more than she did when she was arrested in Hazelton. The Royal Canadian Mounted Police would never have permitted a lone, inexperienced woman to take such a journey in a flimsy boat. If, on the other hand, she was going to Eagle, she would have been expected; if she had failed to arrive, there would have been some notice in the newspaper about it. She must have had a specific destination between Dawson and Eagle where she had arranged to meet her man. He would have left to go back to his traplines just as soon as the ice broke up.

That is why the Mounties permitted her to go.

A coherent explanation for Lillian's disappearance begins to take shape. Sometime in October 1928, Lillian had taken up with a prospector-cum-trapper by the name of Smith, who had come into Dawson City for the winter. In early May, when the Yukon ice broke up, he had returned to his traplines in the vast wilderness of the top of the world that straddles the Canada–Alaska border. A month later, when Lillian left in her flimsy craft with no supplies, she had a planned rendezvous with this man farther down the river. They lived together in isolation, trapping and prospecting in various places in northwestern Alaska, eventually moving south to Skagway and finally the milder climate of the islands of the Inside Passage. Fifty years after leaving Dawson, Lillian Smith died in Sitka, aged eighty-three. This narrative has a pleasing logic to it and a sense of closure.

As I gaze out my window at the kaleidoscope of cloud created by the rising sun, a phrase, from *The Great Gatsby* I think, floats into my mind.

Isn't it pretty to think so.

By the time I am sitting upright with my tray-table stowed and seat belt fastened, I can think of nothing but seeing my husband again. I squeeze my eyes tight to conjure his handsome, weathered face.

There is little traffic at the Sydney international airport and I get through immigration and customs in a trice. Shouldering my backpack, I sprint into the arrival concourse to where Michael stands a good head above most of the waiting throng.

I fling myself at him.

"Nothing else matters," I say breathlessly, my face pressed against his chest. "Nothing else matters except that I love you and I will never leave you for so long again."

"Too right," he says, reaching around me to lever the pack off my back. "You and me, happily ever after."

Isn't that how all the best stories end?